Ireland:
A nation in transition

Ireland:
A nation in transition

Wole Akande

Writers Club Press
San Jose New York Lincoln Shanghai

Ireland: A nation in transition

Writers Club Press
an imprint of iUniverse.com, Inc.

For information address:
iUniverse.com, Inc.
5220 S 16th, Ste. 200
Lincoln, NE 68512
www.iuniverse.com

ISBN: 0-595-19201-7

Printed in the United States of America

To my parents who sacrificed so much for
my education and my wife for her forbearance

Contents

PREFACE

May 2001.

In this age of globalisation with scores of developing countries struggling with poverty and economic deprivation, Ireland's transition from a stumbling agrarian country into one of the world's most lavishly successful service-sector economies within a decade is a beacon of hope in a world of despair. The Irish republic today is a far cry from Ireland of the early 1980s when output was stagnant. Unemployment, which approached 20% in the 80s, is now down to 4%, and the debilitating, centuries-old emigration trend has been shunted into reverse. In the most startling development, Ireland is now the world's biggest exporter of computer software, nudging ahead of America for the first time last year.

Far from being a nation finally at peace with itself and comfortable with its newfound affluence, the "Celtic Tiger" Ireland seems increasingly fraught with contradictions. There can be little doubt that Ireland has made a giant leap towards becoming a secular state over the past decade: contraception is now freely available, limited divorce is finally on the statute books and the influence of the church largely destroyed by sex scandals in the early 90s. The country is now predominantly urban, with two-thirds of the population living in towns and cities, a negative image of the 30s and 40s, when De Valera (Ireland's first president and guiding spiritual father) forged his vision of a rural priest-ridden Catholic wonderland, populated by athletic farm-boys and comely maidens dancing at the crossroads.

Yet, almost by sheer force of habit, much of the old order remains. This is still the only country in Europe to outlaw abortion, the only country in the world with this ban written into its constitution. In an act of collective moral doublethink, it appears that there is widespread tolerance of the fact that over 6,000 Irish women travel every year to Britain for the operation, an alarmingly high percentage in late-term because of the lack of support and advice at home.

The Celtic Tiger economic boom was essentially created not by the Irish but by American hi-tech multinationals, eager to find a convenient launch-pad into Europe and attracted to Ireland by its educated and moderately rewarded workforce, Euro-friendly orientation, and crucially, by its rock-bottom rate of corporate tax. To date, no other single factor has done quite so much to undermine the rhetoric of the boom than the constant revelations flowing from tribunals set up to investigate massive wrongdoing by the political and business elite in the 70s, 80s and early 90s. Irish politics (it appears) is now not merely tainted by corruption, but characterised by it. By far the most disturbing aspect of this corruption is the reluctance to punish any of the culprits. To date, none of the major protagonists has been imprisoned or even fined.

I lived and worked in Ireland from 1998-2001; Ireland has proved to be by far the most confounding and at the same time the most engaging place I have visited. During my residence in the country I made regular contributions to both the electronic and print media on various topical issues. Eventually, the Irish Examiner, one of the three major newspapers in the country, offered me a weekly opinion column. In this book, I have compiled a selection of my writings on the topical issues that capture the essence of the transition being made by the Emerald Isle, as the Irish Republic moves into the 21st century.

INTRODUCTION

The recent announcement that an Indian Company Zoom Technologies intends to employ 150 people in Dublin within the next year is the most significant news item I can recall since I first arrived in Ireland in 1998. Fifteen years ago who would have ever imagined that a company from a developing country would be providing high tech jobs in Europe's fastest growing economy?

Obviously, it is a great understatement to say, "Ireland is going through a period of great transition." With the prospect of peace in the North and the unprecedented Irish economic boom, the world can hardly fail to notice the Irish success story.

Like many Nigerians and other Africans presently residing in Ireland, I walked into Shannon Airport with a considerable amount of ignorance about my new country of employment and residence.

For many Africans, the two enduring images of Ireland stem principally from the Troubles, which contrast starkly with the Christian kindness shown by Irish Catholic missionaries in Africa.

Years ago, as a young boy in southwestern Nigeria attending a Convent school established by Irish Catholic Sisters, I had no idea that I would eventually find my way to Ireland. However, it is a testament to the quality of the early education I received at that Convent school that it formed the bedrock of my professional training, initially in Law and subsequently in software engineering.

All over the African continent, the selfless work of Irish missionaries in the fields of education, health and community development is clearly visible and a credit to the philanthropy of the Irish people who have supported their work over the years.

While working in London, I was fortunate enough to meet and work with quite a few London based Irish. Many were first generation immigrants to England and they were very friendly and understanding about what it means to live in a new and somewhat strange environment.

On arrival in Limerick, my wife and I would have suffered from severe isolation and loneliness, were it not for the helpfulness and kindness of professional colleagues, neighbours and the local people generally. In the two months prior to my wife's arrival in Limerick, not knowing any other Nigerian in Limerick or any other part of Ireland, I was forced to make expensive international phone calls, anytime I felt like speaking my native language.

With the onset of the Government's asylum seekers dispersal scheme, I have seen the same understanding and welcoming spirit in the selfless work of several anonymous local volunteers in Galway (where I marched with asylum seekers invited to participate in the St. Patrick's day celebration), Glengariff, West Cork, and also in Limerick where I have joined other volunteers to prepare for the newcomers, soon to be dispersed to that city.

It is unfortunate that certain sections of the media have tended to focus on the fears of local communities (often not adequately consulted beforehand) and also the flash points where nasty incidents have occurred in the on going dispersal process. However, that is not to say that there are no real issues of tolerance and acceptance of diversity and pluralism.

Earlier this month, I felt saddened when I read about the latest racial attack on a Nigerian shop in Parnell Street and the subsequent closure of the only Nigerian restaurant in Ireland, which was situated on the same street. As a previous recipient of racially motivated hate mail myself, I can understand how African shop owners in Dublin feel when they continually receive racially motivated threats and violent acts of intimidation.

While I realise that the Government is grappling with a relatively unprecedented issue, its piecemeal policies are not helping matters.

The details of the dispersal policy have been shrouded in unnecessary secrecy, not only from local communities receiving asylum seekers but also from established voluntary groups willing to assist both the Government and refugees.

The rationale of effectively making asylum seekers dependant on the government's so called full board "direct provision" arrangements, when labour shortages are hindering the future growth of the fast growing economy is an expensive anomaly.

There is a stark contrast between the enthusiasm and great desire of most asylum seekers (that I have met) to contribute their quota to Irish society as opposed to the perception in some quarters that they have come to scrounge from the social welfare system.

Frankly, in the present atmosphere, it is difficult to see how effective social integration and development of a truly multi cultural Irish society will develop, if we continue to lurch from one immigration or refugee crisis to another. On the bright side, the equality legislation formally making discrimination on the basis of race (and other grounds) illegal was eventually signed into law by President Mary McAleese earlier this month. Working through the National Consultative Committee on Racism, the Government has promised a public awareness campaign to combat growing racism and xenophobia, later this year.

Another positive development is RTE's recently launched new multi cultural radio service, aptly named Radio One World.

The newly established Equality Authority is also a step in the right direction with respect to protection against discrimination and the promotion of equal opportunities. Even the gardaí [*Irish police*] is moving along these lines; recently there was a garda conference on interculturalism and diversity.

Looking to the future, my personal experience of speaking to transition year students about multi cultural diversity on behalf of the Midwest Development Education Agency has been very positive indeed.

Obviously, there is a considerable way to go and resistance to change and acceptance of new cultures is always perceptible, especially by those who are visibly different, but a start has been made and it's a step in the right direction.

In many ways Ireland is very lucky. We are only at the beginning of this process of interculturalism but we can learn from the experiences of other European countries.

With the opportunity given to me to work legitimately, my personal experience to date in Ireland has been a positive and happy one. On that basis, I remain convinced that Irish society will be greatly enriched if the opportunity that I have been given is extended to others. In the English Midlands, Ugandan (Asian) refugees from East Africa have created over 30,000 jobs, on that basis, who can truly compute the potential beneficial value of the new immigrants to the Irish nation in the not too distant future? **23 May 2000**

CHALLENGE OF COSMOPOLITANISM

The Chamber of Commerce's stinging criticism, last Friday, of the Government's work permit and immigration policy continues to demonstrate the difficulties faced by employers seeking to fill vacancies in vital industries. This is despite the much publicised requirement, recommended by the £40 billion National Development Plan, to employ 200,000 extra workers from overseas by 2006.

Speaking with RTÉ, Mr. Simon Nugent, of the Chamber of Commerce, described the system as chaotic. At present, four different Government departments are involved in processing work permits. He explained that his members felt bedeviled by a heap of bureaucracy: "They describe the system as labyrinthine, complex, a maze. There are, in practice, several systems, depending on the sector, and a plethora of rules."

It is sadly ironic that despite the introduction of a limited fast track procedure for employing foreign workers (after months of deliberations), and four FA'S [*Irish Government Employment Agency*] job fairs in as many countries, the net effect of the Government's tweaking with the convoluted immigration system has been inconsequential. Despite an EU commissioned report indicating that foreign workers will become imperative in order to counter the declining birth rate and ageing population in Europe, the Government has been slow to respond to what is likely to become an unavoidable issue. How do we attract the workers we need if we can't find them locally?

1

It is instructive to note that over the last 12 months Britain, Germany, the US and Japan have been busy liberalising their work permit requirements and regulations. The knock on effect of these changes will only make our foreign recruitment drive an uphill task.

The pool of available overseas workers who have the desired skills may be shrinking. After almost three decades of promoting a zero immigration policy the German government found it excruciatingly difficult to attract Indian computer professionals when it introduced its green card scheme for foreign workers earlier this year.

During a visit to India this year, Germany's Foreign Minister, Joschka Fischer, was startled to find that the chief minister of Karnataka, India' s most hi tech state, was too busy to meet him. During a trip to Bangalore, Mr. Fischer called on Azim Premji, the head of the Indian software giant Wipro and the richest man on the subcontinent. Mr Premji told him the scheme was bureaucratic and unworkable. Instead, he suggested, Germany should think about introducing a flexible system of short-term visas for software professionals.

A viable short-term solution to the employment shortage in this country would be to extend the work authorisation scheme introduced earlier this year. They should then integrate its administration, along with all other immigration matters, under one single Government agency.

The new work authorisation rules allow nurses, IT and construction professionals, from countries outside the European economic area, to apply for a work visa from the nearest Irish embassy or consulate. However, the visa is obtainable only on production of a valid job offer from an Irish employer. The other system—which applies to all other work categories—entails an employer finding the worker, applying for a work permit and informing the job candidate, who must then apply for a visa.

Once they have a visa, immigrants under both systems have to present themselves at an immigration point. Even at this point, an immigration officer can still use his or her discretion to refuse the immigrant entry.

Furthermore, the new system applies to nurses but not to doctors; to software programmers but not to fund managers; to quantity surveyors, but not to bricklayers and labourers. Chefs, waiters and kitchen porters need the old work permit. Seasonal farm workers remain under the old system also.

Curiously, existing work permit holders cannot benefit from the new, more liberal rules. The updated work permit rules apply only to new applicants. Existing work permit holders have seen very little liberalisation in rules on work permits, immigration and residence procedures.

These are three different areas of the same problem and each must be addressed if the stated policy to facilitate economically related immigration is to have effect. Significantly, the most vehement advocates for change have been Irish people returning from abroad. People who have encountered irrational, bureaucratic and inexplicable rules for immigration, residence and work permit applying to their non-Irish friends and prospective spouses.

At the FA'S job fair in South Africa, it was announced there are over 40,000 immediate job vacancies in this country.

Those who have argued for strong immigration controls must now demonstrate why a liberal, open system cannot work better. The economy needs it, our society benefits. Many of the controls—such as signing on at police stations annually—cannot possibly be effective and are nothing more than a wasteful, bureaucratic annoyance.

If we were to design an immigration system from scratch for the start of the 21st century, it would be nothing like the one we have now.

It is vital that this Government now facilitates an interdepartmental integration of all immigration related administration. Hopefully, this will remove many of the inconsistencies and hindrances that plague the system, whilst at the same time prepare the basis for the formulation of a modern and imaginative immigration policy in line with the nation's economic requirements. **5th December 2000**

*   *   *

Let America show us how to open doors to equality

Equality of opportunity, irrespective of colour or creed, is perhaps the greatest gift that only a country as diverse as the United States of America can bestow upon the rest of the world. The nomination of three citizens from minority groups to the highest political offices in that country is confirmation of this fact.

In view of the unhealthy divisions caused by the disputed presidential elections that thrust George W Bush into the White House, it was not too surprising that last Saturday the US President elect enjoyed milking the symbolism of being able to name the first black man to occupy the country's highest diplomatic post. The move was his first official cabinet appointment.

Although his nomination to the office of the US Secretary of State was a deliberate break with the new President elect's Republican party' s tradition of catering exclusively to an affluent all white elite, retired General Colin Powell and the two other ethnic minorities nominees are no strangers to high public office. At the press conference announcing his appointment the General made explicit reference to the colour of his skin and his humble origins in the Bronx, New York, saying his career trajectory should be an inspiration to African Americans. He also paid tribute to the civil rights struggle without which his rise in the ranks of the US army would have been impossible.

Of course, cherry picking a few visibly different faces to high office is no guarantee of real change in society. It is important to guard against tokenism or symbolism. But it is a significant step and a marker in the opening up and liberalisation of a diverse and multi ethnic society.

Ireland has become increasingly cosmopolitan within a very short period of time. This is the reality and the challenge we face. It is a challenge that requires a great deal of imaginative leadership.

Earlier this month, after an inexplicable six month delay, the Government finally announced its appointments to the Human Rights

Commission. The commission was established to promote and monitor human rights in the State.

Amazingly only one of eight commissioners recommended by an independent selection committee set up by the Government was eventually appointed. Among those recommended but not appointed were representatives of the Traveller movement and the Irish Commission for Prisoners Overseas.

Inez McCormack, president of Irish Congress of Trade Unions (ICTU), who was a member of the independent selection committee, hit the nail on the head when she explained: "The issue is this. That if those who need change are not regarded ultimately as able to be fit to sit at the table, then we have a fatally flawed process."

Donncha O' Connell, Director of Irish Council for Civil Liberties (ICCL), responded similarly: "The real victims in all of this are people with disabilities, Travellers and other minorities who have been sidelined in this vital new infrastructure for human rights in the Republic."

In Britain, and other neighbouring countries with more established ethnic communities, members of minority groups are routinely appointed to publicly funded commissions charged with the protection of human rights. The impact of such diverse representation goes far beyond vague notions of cosmopolitan symbolism. It has the potential to minimise societal marginalisation by highlighting and resolving pressing grievances specific to peripheral groups within existing civil institutions. Above all, it makes for a more inclusive and enriched society that will benefit all.

Other multi ethnic societies have witnessed street riots and ghettoisation on the road to creating a more inclusive society. However, I see no reason why we, as an emerging multi cultural society, have to go down the same path.

Although Government continues to take a slow and cautious pace in these matters, the populace of this country has demonstrated a more open approach to minorities than they have been given credit for. For instance, I will be surprised if the Refugee Council does not make thousands from proceeds of the sale of the recently launched refugee support badge being sold at several Body Shop outlets.

I have heard some commentators talk about the people of this country not being ready for cosmopolitanism and a multiracial society. I find such views difficult to accept in view of the recognition that this society has previously conferred on distinguished members of the ethnic community.

With the exception of the British parliament at Westminster, very few European parliaments have any ethnic minority members. Yet despite this trend, eight years ago, when there were far fewer ethnic people in this country than we have at the moment, the first Muslim, Dr Moosajee Bhamjee, was elected to Dáil.

Former President Mary Robinson (and UN Commissioner for Human Rights) has criticised the appointments process for the new Human Rights Commission as not being open and transparent. Mrs Robinson has also indicated that she would have detailed discussions with Mr O'Donoghue this week on the Human Rights Commission.

It was also reported that the chairman of the commission, Mr Justice Donal Barrington, threatened to resign last week on this same issue but withdrew his resignation after receiving undertakings from Minister for Justice Mr O' Donoghue. In order to defuse the situation, there are suggestions that Mr O'Donoghue is to propose increasing the membership of the commission from eight to at least 12.

Although this is likely to require legislative change the least the Minister can do at this late stage would be to ensure that the four additional human rights commissioners include representatives of the most vulnerable and disadvantaged sections of the community.

By making these crucial amendments, this would ensure that those who were sidelined in the initial appointment process, namely people with disabilities, Travellers and ethnic minorities are fully involved in our future.

19ᵗʰ December 2000

*   *   *

Updated Immigration Bill should pave the way to a fairer system for all

At last the Government is on the verge of releasing details of the proposed Immigration and Residence Bill 2001, which will replace the 65 year old Aliens Act of 1935. Although few details are known at this stage, it is clear the Bill will set out to modernise procedures for the issue of visas and residence permits. It will also re define immigrants' rights in relation to basics, like healthcare, education, training and housing.

Broadly speaking the procedures will facilitate legal immigration. This implies that issues relating to asylum seekers will remain outside its remit. Obviously asylum problems must be managed with asylum tools and migration problems with migration tools. However, the ease with which those in authority and the media interchangeably use the terms asylum seeker and illegal immigrant demonstrates the immediate associations made between the two.

When the door of legal immigration is (for practical purposes) firmly shut on those from poorer nations, is it surprising that economic migrants from the developing world knock on the asylum door instead?

Although monthly statistics for asylum seekers are readily available from the Department of Justice, figures for those seeking entry visas to this country from overseas are difficult to come by. I would surmise that Irish statistics would be broadly in line with the British figures.

In 1997, 0.49% of US citizens requesting settlement in Britain were denied entry. The figure for the Indian subcontinent was 29%. In the same year, while only 0.18% of Australian visitors' applications were refused, the refusal rate for Ghanaian applications was over 30%.

As long as migratory pressure meets with a disproportionate response from a receiving country, ambitious or desperate migrants the two are not always easy to tell apart will consider other means of entry.

It is easy to fall into the sanctimonious trap of bemoaning those who apparently misuse the asylum process, conveniently forgetting the inconsistencies with which western governments have long classified new arrivals. In the 1950s, when many continental western European economies were booming, de facto refugees from fascist Spain and Portugal were welcomed as economic migrants because the host countries, including Britain, needed their labour. During the Cold War, economic migrants from communist countries were allowed in as political refugees to score points against Communism and the defunct Soviet Union.

Today, a different sort of inconsistency appears. For example, a young Greek, as a citizen of the European Union, can walk into any Dublin shop and ask for a job, no matter how menial. A young Turk needs a work permit, which will be issued only if an employer certifies that his or her skills cannot be found locally in this country. A young Kosovan is banned from working at all and forced to rely on £15 per week comfort money. Yet all three may have the same skills and the same command of English language and to Irish eyes may look identical.

The point of such distinctions is mainly to reduce the flow of foreigners across our borders. Last year saw a significant tightening up of asylum procedures in an attempt to discourage misuse and speed up the processing of asylum applications. Under the Direct Provision Scheme, newly arrived asylum seekers no longer have the option of living in private rented accommodation and receiving social welfare payments of £72 per week. Instead, they are housed in full board accommodation in hostels, hotels and B&Bs, with laundry facilities provided. They receive £15 comfort money per week per adult and £7.50 per child.

Powers to detain and fingerprint asylum seekers took effect in November when the Refugee Act 1996 became law, complementing already existing Garda powers to detain failed asylum seekers. Furthermore, readmission agreements are being negotiated with Nigeria and Poland, and have already been signed with Romania, which will fast track the deportation of failed asylum applicants. Already there are reports that the numbers of asylum seekers arriving in the State are beginning to decline.

This is a radical change from a few months ago when repeated calls for amnesty for asylum seekers were rejected. With the opportunities presented by the introduction of the Immigration and Residence Bill 2001, now is the time for the Government to reconsider allowing asylum seekers to have an automatic right to work six months after arriving in the country.

The reality is that despite substantial staff increases in the asylum processing area, the six-month average target period for processing applications has not been achieved. Moreover, asylum seekers in other EU countries (including Britain) have a right to work after a minimum prescribed period.

In the present environment, where employers and recruitment agencies are desperately seeking skilled workers (that are, in many instances, not readily available locally), it seems an awful waste of resources to allow asylum seekers to live a life of idleness. A few months ago I heard of a case of a Nigerian doctor in Ennis who was unable to work simply because he is an asylum seeker. There are hospitals all over the country desperately in need of medical staff.

Regrettably, his case is not unique. In Limerick, the professions represented among asylum seekers dispersed to that city include nurses, teachers, mechanical engineers, electricians, bankers, truck drivers and tillers. The recent case of the Filipino nurse, who (despite being employed legally) was allegedly exploited by recruiters, has highlighted the need to avoid unwittingly creating a black economy for low paid jobs where illegal, undocumented persons are employed at the mercy of unscrupulous businessmen.

Obviously, it is also indefensible to deprive the poorest countries of those with the most skills. It is said there are more doctors from Sierra Leone in Chicago than in the country itself.

But these brain drain arguments tend to prove marginal when looked at more closely. In a way, migrant communities prove a far more potent and effective way of helping the developing world than official overseas aid policies.

The IMF estimated at the beginning of the 1990s that the global value of remittances sent home by migrant workers totaled $65bn a year some $20bn more than the official global overseas aid effort. **2nd January 2001**

*   *   *

Xenophobia cannot be tolerated further

The publication of the Christmas statement by the Four Catholic Bishops warning against xenophobia (December 24, 1999) highlights the "untold consequences for already vulnerable" victims of such racial harassment, a much more unpleasant and potentially dangerous variation of racial discrimination.

In the present tense climate with "racist leaflets being pushed through doors", walls being daubed with insulting racist graffiti, coupled with increasing incidents of "racially motivated intimidation or violence", threatening phonecalls, verbal abuse and especially with the offices of Association of Refugees and Asylum Seekers being 'abandoned' for three weeks last November after being threatened with arson, there can be no doubt that the warning against racial harassment by the four bishops, is justified and timely.

What is especially worrying in the last 12 months, has been the reluctance or inability of the Gardaí to curb the more extreme racist incidents by prosecuting the racist offenders, including the individuals who sent racially motivated hate mail to the Lord Mayor of Dublin, earlier this year.

Criminal prosecution under the wide-ranging provisions of the Incitement to Hatred legislation could effectively be utilised by the Gardaí to address the specific examples of racist harassment raised by the four bishops.

Personally, I am not aware of any attempt by the Gardaí to prosecute, or enforce the full rigour of the laws against suspected racist offenders.

Perhaps the Gardaí are hampered by the present legislative deficit in Ireland?

While we have the Incitement to Hatred legislation, the Employment Equality Act and the Equal Status Bill now being steered through the Oireachtas [Irish Parliament], there is a legislative deficit in creating the sort of environment common to other host countries. Nowhere in the Constitution, for example, is racial discrimination specifically outlawed. Surprisingly, Ireland is the only EU country that has not yet ratified the 30-year-old UN Convention on the Elimination of All Forms of Discrimination.

Even more disturbing is the manner the promised Garda investigation into the blatantly unlawful denial of entry into Ireland (apparently on racial grounds) of two visiting British citizens of Ghanaian origin by Garda officers, on October 14, after they arrived by ferry at Dún Laoghaire from Britain (The Examiner, November 18) has been conveniently swept under the carpet and forgotten.

With the Government quietly proceeding with dispersal of refugees despite reservations expressed by all the relevant groups, it is not too late for the Gardaí to adopt a more pro active and progressive approach to policing in race related incidents. For starters the Gardaí may consider embracing the spirit of an anti racism code of practice, recently drawn up by black and minority ethnic groups, asylum seekers and traveller organisations, (under an umbrella body, United Against Racism) through an anti racist sub group of the Community Development Programmes National Advisory Committee.

In conclusion, there is an imperative need to send a clear and unambiguous signal to individuals or groups involved in organised racial harassment that they will be punished in accordance with the law and they could suffer severe legal consequences themselves, if they continue their nefarious and illegal activities. **5th January 2000**

*   *   *

MOVING TOWARDS PLURALISM

With the constant news of negative developments for refugees and other foreigners living in Ireland, it is often difficult not to be despondent about the prospects of a multicultural society. Fortunately, work towards achieving a more pluralist society is slowly progressing in a quiet but significant way with the potential to improve the lives of both old and new minorities and also to enrich mainstream Irish society with a diversity that previously was unthinkable. A case in point is RTÉ's recently launched new multicultural radio service, aptly named "Radio One World", which is being presented by Paulina Chiwangu and Marcus Connaughton. The new service includes news from abroad and from Ireland in the various languages required, English lessons for those new to the language, and arts programming from RTÉ's main channels. The newly established Equality Authority is also a step in the right direction with respect to protection against discrimination and the promotion of equal opportunities. Even the Garda is moving along these lines and significantly the Garda Commissioner, Mr Pat Byrne, at the Garda conference on "Inter cultural-ism and Diversity", announced that ethnic minorities are to have an increased input into Garda training. Obviously, there is a considerable way to go and resistance to change and acceptance of new cultures is always perceptible, especially by those who are visibly different in this country, but a start has been made and it's a step in the right direction. In many ways Ireland is very lucky. We are only at the beginning of this process but we can learn from the experiences of other European countries. It is essential that Irish society does not lose this opportunity. **10th April 2000**

*   *   *

Prosperity relies on foreign labour

The latest forecast by Goodbody Stockbrokers (The Examiner, February 28th) on the booming economy is undoubtedly good news. But, once again, it raises the need for a liberal immigration policy to attract, at least, 20,000 foreign workers to maintain the economy for another three years.

It appears that the crucial link between this country's future prosperity and the establishment of an immigration policy that attracts much needed foreign workers (to fill labour shortages in key industries such as construction and the computer software) has not been properly established in the public consciousness.

The dithering of the Government in formulating and executing a liberal immigration policy for foreign workers only serves to postpone the inevitable while far right groups, like the Immigration Control Platform, continue their scare mongering campaigns against present and future immigrants.

The invaluable input of foreign doctors in the health service is well recognised. Many of these doctors come from my home country, Nigeria, an English speaking country, which, unfortunately, is in the middle of an economic recession.

There are thousands of well-educated Nigerian professionals and graduates who would be willing to travel to work in Ireland under an appropriate immigration policy.

It is generally accepted that the work permit system is far too restrictive to attract the numbers of foreign workers presently needed.

Obviously part of the problem is the prevailing unenthusiastic attitude towards the few thousands of immigrants seeking asylum in Ireland. The Government continues to insist that the majority of the applicants are economic migrants.

Now that foreign workers are required to keep the economy booming, certainly there is some merit in the institution of an immigration policy that allows Irish embassies abroad (for instance Nigeria) to issue work visas to suitably skilled applicants. Surely this would go a long way to resolving the refugee crisis that is being needlessly prolonged by the Government at Irish taxpayers' expense. **4th March 2000**

"CÉAD MÍLE FÁILTE" —REFUGE IN THE LAND OF A "THOUSAND WELCOMES"

In a country where the presumption of innocence is guaranteed for those charged with the most serious criminal offences, it is ironic that any law would effectively take away similar guarantees to those arriving to our shores.

Yesterday, the full implementation of the amended Refugee Act 1996 became effective. The Act enables the State to take the fingerprints of all asylum seekers over the age of 14.

If they should refuse (and are over the age of 18) they can be detained. If Gardaí or immigration officers suspect they have unreasonably destroyed their identity documents, or are carrying forged ones, they can also be detained.

The power to detain newly arrived asylum seekers on six grounds compliments existing garda powers to hold failed asylum seekers prior to deportation. The major changes being that immigration officers or gardaí now have what are effectively preventive detention powers.

A garda or immigration officer who suspects that a person will not comply with a deportation order has the power to detain that person for up to eight weeks. This opens up the possibility that individuals may be detained despite the fact they have not committed any unlawful act.

This new power may be contrary to European and international human rights law. The detention of asylum seekers in the UK and Australia has already been criticised by United Nations Human Rights bodies.

Moreover, the Act also reduces to 14 days the time limit within which asylum seekers can seek a judicial review of decisions refusing an application for asylum. Usually, three months are given for such applications. It is thought that a time limit of 14 days will be unworkable.

Given that asylum seekers have been continually stigmatised and criminalised by our government and law enforcement agencies, I wouldn't blame anyone who seeks to steer well clear of asylum seekers. However, it is astonishing how the common bonds and fraternity that we share as human beings transcend even the most draconian laws.

Last week, residents of Tramore, Co Waterford, began a campaign to stop the threatened deportation of a Nigerian woman whose application for asylum failed. A rally is to be held in the town next Saturday, in support of Ms Ebi Ojoh, who has been living in Tramore with two of her children, a boy aged 15 and a girl aged 8, since June. Ms Ojoh, who claims her life would be in danger if she was forced to return home, says her children have settled well in local schools and are worried about the future.

"My kids are so happy here. The people are very friendly. They stop you in the street, smile and say hello. It's very comforting."

Ms Ojoh says her application for asylum was dealt with under the fast track procedure and rejected. Her appeal against the decision has also been turned down. Her only remaining option is to apply to the Minister for Justice to be allowed to stay on humanitarian grounds. If it fails, she faces deportation.

Speaking for the fundraising committee that was set up to fight Ms Ojoh's case last week, chairwoman Ms Alison Tuohy said she had got to know Ms Ojoh because they had children in the same school. She said a lot of negativity had come out of Tramore when it was first suggested that asylum seekers would be accommodated in the area. "Now is the time to redeem ourselves."

Ms Ojoh told the meeting her life in Ireland was not as comfortable as in Nigeria, but she had had to leave. She was a member of the Ijaw ethnic group, which was being oppressed by other ethnic groups. Two of her brothers had been killed and she had decided to leave when her partner and elder son were taken from their home. She claimed that while the Nigerian government stated everything was normal, fighting had gone underground which made things more dangerous than before.

"I'm living below zero compared to what I used to know, because I was really comfortable. But now I have peace."

Ms Ojo sold her shop in order to pay for her flight from Nigeria, but many others did not have the means. She paid somebody to get her out but did not know where she was going until she arrived in Dublin on a flight from Lagos. Within days she was transferred to an accommodation centre in Tramore.

The helpful response by Tramore residents to asylum seekers is not unique. Despite the lack of consultation with local communities by the Government in the execution of its much criticised asylum dispersal policy earlier in the year, there is hardly any town or village in this country with asylum seekers that does not have a refugee support group. By and large these groups are not state funded and consist of local volunteers, ordinary people concerned about the plight of the strangers in the midst. In many remote villages and towns, the contribution of such groups to the integration of asylum seekers in the community has been invaluable.

It is not hard to imagine how it must feel to arrive in a strange country, before being put on a coach to an unknown destination to live in regimented accommodation on £15 a week, with nothing to do but wait for a distant authority to determine your fate. In these circumstances, the value of a friendly face, a helping hand, a local guide, a translator, cannot be quantified. One Cork based asylum seeker writes: "To be a foreigner is hard, people generally think of the pain of nostalgia; but what's worst is the pain of estrangement. When everything becomes new, unknown, strange, difficult; finding places or someone helping, supporting, it could be like light in the darkness of the winter night."

Given that so many people in this country are so generous with their time and resources, it is baffling that the Government considers it necessary to adopt extreme measures in the pursuit of its asylum policy. This is especially so when one considers that the numbers arriving here are rather small when compared with the numbers of asylum seekers in neighbouring countries. If the monthly figures released over the summer are reliable, those numbers may actually be slowing down.

Now that all elements of this controversial law are fully applicable, the least the Government can do is to establish the Refugee Advisory Board recommended by the same law.

By appointing persons who represent the interests of refugees and asylum seekers, and who have knowledge of asylum and the provision of protection, the more severe aspects of the law will be implemented in a humane and compassionate manner that is more representative of the humanity and kindness that has been exhibited by ordinary people throughout the length and breadth of this country. **21st November 2000**

*   *   *

It's wrong to punish children for the actions of parents

Nothing is more painful than the removal of a legal right or entitlement. That being the case, it is difficult to understand why any government or law should seek to strip four or five year old children of citizenship that was previously bestowed on them through the due process of law?

Unbelievable as it sounds, this is the intention and net effect of the amendment proposed by the Immigration Control Platform (ICP) to section three of the Irish Nationality and Citizenship Bill. Thankfully, the

Dáil committee dealing with the relevant section of the Bill last Wednesday did not take the amendment on board. However, the group insists that it will seek to have its amendment (withdrawing automatic citizenship from children under the age of six of failed asylum seekers and illegal immigrants) considered at the report stage of the Bill.

Proposing further immigration restrictions on adult newcomers during an economic boom with labour shortages may be debatable. But effectively punishing innocent children for the alleged misdemeanours of their parents is appalling. The direct effect of the proposal will render the young children stateless and possibly liable for deportation. Not only does the proposition challenge well established constitutional guarantees to children and family life in this country, it's a clear illustration of the very sort of chauvinism that negates the more pluralistic and cosmopolitan society that Ireland is fast becoming.

According to the organisation, Ireland is the only EU country that automatically confers citizenship on all children born on the Island. But the reality is moving in the opposite direction. Many EU countries are seeking to liberalise their immigration and nationality laws.

Last year, after 86 years, Germany got rid of the very same nationality laws that the ICP is proposing when Gerhard Schroder's centre left coalition introduced laws to break the bond between blood and nationality. It allows foreigners to become citizens after living in Germany for eight years providing they give up their existing passport. Children who have been born in Germany of foreign parents can keep dual citizenship, but are obliged to choose which to keep by the age of 23.

In France, children born in France of foreign parents are entitled to French citizenship. Last year the Labour government in Britain announced a concession to grant residence (and eventually citizenship) to families of illegal immigrants with dependent children aged seven years or older. The position in the United States is well known and is exactly the same as this country.

At the root of the extreme views of anti immigrant organisations like the ICP is a wilful fear of diversity and the erroneous view that cultural diversity is threatening. At a time when immigration has overtaken emigration for the first time in the history of this country, such views are not only unfortunate but also patently unhelpful.

Building a multicultural society will never be a bed of roses. Tensions still exist in long established multicultural communities across the Atlantic like Los Angeles and New York. Across the Irish Sea, in London (where over 300 languages are spoken daily) lessons are still being learnt about the ramifications of policing in a multicultural environment.

Naturally, it takes time to break barriers and promote better mutual understanding across communities. But the need for a fair and forward-looking legal framework is paramount. Experiences in other countries have shown that diversity does not have to be threatening. It is possible to build understanding and mutual tolerance. Furthermore, children born in Ireland today are the seeds of a future inclusive and diverse community, whatever their cultural heritage. Ireland remains the country of their birth and no law can take that away from them.

Of course, there are those who will always abuse the system. But while such abuse cannot be condoned, extremist organisations cannot be allowed to set the agenda. Although there is a possibility of abuse, the withdrawal of nationality to infants will not resolve the crisis the Government is grappling with in implementing its refugee and asylum policy.

For many people, the ultimate proof of nationality and citizenship is in the acquiring and holding of a passport relating to their country of residence. Last month the Irish Independent asked why 15% of the population (600,000 Irish men and women), most of whom are voters, hold British passports.

The answer is obvious. They are entitled to do so, like Irish born children of foreign parents, simply by circumstance of their birth.

Although Ireland has been a sovereign and independent country since 1922, any person born here before 1949 is entitled to British nationality by law. Passport records at the British embassy in Dublin show that it's an entitlement that is not disregarded. The embassy is kept busy renewing over 70,000 British passports annually. Just imagine the public outcry in this country if the British parliament stripped all Irish holders of their British passports overnight at the stroke of a pen.

Of course, British nationality is not the only foreign nationality that Irish citizens have inherited by birth. Last month, while I was trying to renew my passport at the Nigerian embassy, I met an Irish lady who was there for the same purpose.

She was also enquiring about Nigerian passport applications for her Irish children, as well as a visiting visa for her Irish husband. Interestingly her Nigerian citizenship was acquired at birth, through her father, a naturalised citizen who still resides in Nigeria.

Many countries worldwide have found that granting citizenship to immigrants is the best way to secure their allegiance and reap their full potential. For an immigrant, there is no greater pride than citizenship and the symbolism of full acceptance by the host community that citizenship conveys.

However, it should be remembered that children born in this country to foreign parents are not immigrants. Obviously they have had no say about their preferred country of birth. Young and innocent children should not suffer any legal hardship as a result of the circumstances of their parents. **7th November 2000**

*   *   *

Some Nigerians need the option of a new life here

The first anniversary of civilian democratic rule in Nigeria coincided with the recent statistics released by the Department of Justice outlining the abysmally low success rate of asylum applications made by Nigerians here.

Nigerians form the second largest group of asylum seekers in Ireland and the statistics give rise to two major questions:

Firstly, for many non Nigerians, it may be difficult to understand why Nigeria, a fledgling new democracy and a major oil producer, with great potential and a natural leader in the African region should produce so many refugees in Ireland.

Secondly, if there are other legitimate alternative immigration entry routes for Nigerians wishing to travel then why are they concentrating on the asylum route as apparently the main method of entry.

Prior to 1997 only ten Nigerians applied for asylum in Ireland. However according to Joseph Lynch, Ireland's Ambassador to Nigeria, there have been links between Nigeria and Ireland for over a hundred years. From the Fifties onward there is definitely some evidence of Nigerian students attending Trinity College and other universities in Ireland. The Dean of my Faculty at University was a Trinity College alumnus.

From 1993 to 1998, several hundred Nigerians were subjected to arbitrary arrests, extra judicial detentions, and state sanctioned assassination under the brutal military regime of the General Sani Abacha. For many non-Nigerians the execution of world-renowned writer Ken Saro Wiwa and eight other Ogoni activists and the subsequent imprisonment of the present Nigerian President (amongst others) was the zenith of human rights' abuse under this former cruel Nigerian military regime.

Several prominent Nigerian politicians and journalists were exiled in the UK and the US where they vigorously campaigned for a return of democracy to Nigeria—affectionately known as the Giant of Africa. Consequently, few exiled Nigerian politicians could resist the appeal of governance when free elections were held last year. Quite a few exiled politicians were elected into political positions in Nigeria and there was much hope of a national revival. From this point of view it is difficult to explain why Nigerian asylum applications shot up to almost 40% of all asylum applications made in Ireland in 1998—only one year before a new civilian administration was sworn into office in Nigeria. However at the recent conference on asylum seekers held at the University College Dublin, Joesphine Olusola, a Nigerian journalist seeking asylum in Ireland, who came here two and a half years ago when Nigeria was still in the grip of a military dictatorship, said: "People here forget that the people you crossed, the people who persecuted you, are still there. Even if they are no longer in power, they are alive."

Many Nigerians resident in Nigeria itself worry about the upsurge in religious and ethnic violence and crime since the new civilian government assumed power. "In the past year, there has been general lawlessness and chaos in the country," said Segun Ojo a resident of Nigeria's largest city, Lagos, "Ethnic regions and groups have become more militant in their quest for autonomy, more powers, or separatist states."

According to the BBC World Service more than 2,000 have died in ethnic or sectarian violence in Nigeria in the past two years. Recently, in Northern Nigeria religious differences have increasingly turned violent.

"It will be a miracle to begin to see the wonders of democracy instantly. But nothing has changed after a year of democratic governance," said Godwin Obaseki, an economist based in Lagos. "Look at where we're coming from. After more than a decade of army misrule; our social utilities have been wrecked by neglect and decay."

Despite the apparent instability, the turmoil and continued economic downturn in Nigeria, the new civilian administration has moved positively and decisively to recover much needed stolen funds by previous corrupt rulers stashed away in foreign bank accounts.

Accordingly, the democratic regime continues to elicit goodwill in the international community and among many Nigerians. On that basis many foreign governments presently take the view that the grounds on which asylum can be claimed by Nigerians no longer exist.

In the case of Ireland, there is concern in official circles that many Nigerian applicants have arrived from other EU countries, shopping around the best asylum deal.

Unlike many other Western countries that have well established Immigration procedures there is a widespread view that for all practical purposes, claiming asylum is the only route for many Nigerians wishing to travel to Ireland.

Unfortunately, according to Conor O' Briain, a solicitor acting for asylum seekers, the criteria for refugee status under the 1951 Refugee Convention is technical and restrictive. They would not apply for example to a family fleeing a war in fear of getting killed in the general destruction; although clearly refugees in layman's terms, they would have great difficulty being recognised as refugees under the Convention.

He argues further that the narrow nature of the term refugee under the 1951 Convention ignores the reality that political and economic injustices are inextricably linked. It is significant to note that the definition of Programme Refugee as a person who has been invited to Ireland on the basis of a government decision, in response to humanitarian requests from bodies such as the UNHCR, is broader than the restrictive definition of Refuge under the 1951 Convention.

A recent newspaper report stated that despite rejection of Nigerian asylum applications by the Justice department here, the Foreign Affairs department continues to fund a Nigerian based civil rights organisation from its overseas democracy and human rights budget.

Despite the recent well publicised relaxation of the work permit regulations, only specialised professionals are eligible. Although job fairs for Irish jobs have been held in countries as far as Canada, enquiries with FAS [*Irish government Employment Agency*] reveal no plans to hold any such job fair in Nigeria or any African country. Nigerian doctors have been working in various parts of Ireland for years. However it can be difficult it for immediate family members to join skilled immigrants legitimately working in Ireland. Perhaps if the Irish Government favourably considered implementing a visa lottery programme similar to that operated by the US government; or the Points Immigration system operated by Canada, New Zealand or Australia, or the new German Government's new Green card scheme, current skill shortages in vital sectors of the economy would be addressed before long term harm was done to the enviable growth rate of the Celtic Tiger. **June 9th 2000**

GLOBALISATION WITH A HUMAN FACE?

The Government's pledge to increase its aid budget to reach the United Nations target of 0.7% of GNP is a promising gesture to tackle global poverty but it may not be enough. Minister responsible for Overseas Development Assistance, Liz O'Donnell, says the Government is committed to increasing its aid budget.

Although Ireland's budget of almost £200m is below the UN target, the contribution has increased steadily from £40m in 1992.

At first glance the rationale for foreign aid is compelling. We are confronted by vivid TV images from less fortunate parts of the globe on a daily basis. Countless lives have been saved through generous Irish donations and other donors in the Western World, especially in the US.

But the statistics make for depressing reading. Nearly 25% of the world's population lives in extreme poverty on less than the equivalent of $1 a day. They lack basic services such as education and health. To this extent the contribution of Irish Non Government Organisations (NGOs) and Irish aid is invaluable in many parts of the world.

Despite the many positive aspects of foreign aid, to a large extent it is at best a palliative. If you're looking for solutions to the world's problems, don't look to aid.

Otherwise it is difficult to explain why, despite the billions and billions of dollars given in aid to developing countries over the past 50 years, a quarter of the world's population still lives in what under UN terms is severe poverty.

In many parts of the world the situation is getting worse, not better. At present growth rates it will take many African countries 40 years just to regain the incomes they had in the 1970s.

Why doesn't $55 billion in aid each year make a substantial difference? Firstly, the sums concerned, though large, can do little to offset the far greater imbalances in the world economic order where raw commodities exported from developing countries have lost more than 50% of their trade value in the last 15 years.

Secondly, for every dollar given in aid, the banks take back three dollars in interest payments on debt, so poor countries pay far more than they receive.

Often the very same aid supplied by donor countries is passed straight back to the World Bank or IMF in debt servicing payments, leaving poorer countries no means of building their own economies or investing in their people.

The relationship between debt servicing and foreign aid is intertwined in many developing countries. A combination of debt relief and cancellation may be the key to unlocking the growth potential in many developing countries.

At the recent G8 meeting in Japan this issue was discussed but little was agreed in concrete terms. It is difficult to understand how the developing countries debt crisis was ever allowed to become such problem that today it prevents developing nations from spending more on health and education than on interest payments, thereby making reliance on foreign aid imperative.

One way of understanding developing countries debt is to imagine falling behind on credit-card repayments. As the warning letters pile up, the money still does not materialise. Personal bankruptcy looms. Although this is a traumatic process, it does cancel the debts and allows for a fresh start of sorts.

But what if there was no such thing as bankruptcy? The interest charges snowball. The credit card company knows there is no realistic chance of clearing the total amount owed, but demands some form of regular payment all the same. Such is the lot of the world's poorest.

The people of the 41 most impoverished countries spend about $8.6 billion (£5.4 billion) on foreign debt payments each year to avoid being totally shut off from the world's financial community.

At the local level, foreign aid can help break the foreign debt/foreign aid cycle by providing the skills and infrastructure necessary for real development, and in many cases it has done so.

Microcredit unions such as the Grameen Bank in Bangladesh, offer the marginalised a chance to break free from poverty through their own efforts. Training schemes, which spread skills through local communities, empower both present and future generations.

When properly targeted and administered, development assistance can support such grassroots initiatives—particularly important when more traditional state support programmes are cut back to satisfy international donors such as the IMF.

Sadly, however, the great majority of aid given by donor countries has served more selfish ends. Aid continues to be a significant weapon of foreign policy—Israel receives more 'aid' per person than almost any other country, despite being one of the world's 25 richest nations.

Aid can also be a useful political lever, as when the USA gave Egypt a seven billion-dollar debt waiver in return for its support in the 1991 Gulf War. 'Tied' aid has often been used to solve domestic economic problems.

In 1986 the British government forced India to accept 21 Westland W-30 helicopters for offshore oil exploration, at a cost to the British aid budget of £65m.

This saved the ailing Westland Company but was of little use to India, which ended up selling the helicopters back to a British dealer as scrap metal.

Another cause of concern is the open-ended nature of foreign aid. Ever since it was provided under the Marshall Plan after World War II, there have been concerns that it should be provided for a limited period.

OECD countries like The Netherlands received a total of US$14.6 billion in the period 1948-1952. Korea received assistance in the '50s and '60s; so did Taiwan. Two things stood out in this form of aid: it was given for a limited period of time, by a limited number of donors (effectively only one, the USA).

The reverse happened in sub-Saharan Africa after independence. A large number of donors assisted these countries for a long period of time. What started as short-term financial and technical assistance, developed into an institution.

Institutions govern the rules of behaviour of those actors involved in the process and provide predictability. African governments and NGO's are part of the aid institution, like the donor agencies in the rich countries.

This is true for so-called structural assistance or development co-operation, as it is for incidental or humanitarian assistance. Aid is institutionalised and bureaucratised.

Given these failures, maybe we shouldn't lose too much sleep over the dramatic fall in aid levels seen over the past two decades. Indeed, there have been many calls for an end to aid, on the grounds that it has done nothing but lock countries into a cycle of dependency from which they cannot escape.

Yet alongside the abuses, it is important to remember the victories which development assistance has made possible, enabling people to secure basic rights and securities for themselves.

Good foreign aid can break the cycle of dependency; it is up to donor countries like Ireland to use it to that end. **July 29th 2000**

*   *   *

Global loan sharks

It is estimated that up to 20,000 anti globalisation protesters will stage demonstrations against the International Monetary Fund (IMF) and its sister organisation the World Bank this morning as they hold their 55th annual summit meetings in the Czech Republic capital, Prague. For anyone who has lived in any of the 90 developing countries unfortunate enough to seek aid from the IMF, it is not difficult to understand why it is a target for so many protesters.

In many developing countries the role of the IMF has been that of an unaccountable and colonial organisation that has pushed millions into poverty. In economic terms, the IMF is the infamous doctor that prescribes the same drug its structural adjustment program for all patients irrespective of their differing conditions and situation. The IMF has played the role of undertaker in the developing world and forced governments into taking suicidal socio economic measures.

My first exposure to the IMF was in the mid 1980s when my home country, Nigeria, was caught in a recession. There was a national debate about whether the Government should accept an IMF loan with its stringent conditions. Despite widespread public disapproval the military Government eventually accepted the loan. Overnight the national currency lost over 80% of its previous value; thousands of workers were laid off by struggling industries unable to afford imported raw materials. Aside from the obligatory belt tightening, Nigerians were told that the currency devaluation would make our exports more competitive in overseas markets, even though 95% of exports from Nigeria are denominated in US dollars.

Although Nigeria borrowed less than $6 billion in 1985, the country has paid over $15billion and it still owes $28 billion. At this rate, it is obvious that Nigeria will never get out of debt. Most of the country's resources are spent on servicing debt instead of delivering development to the local people.

Corruption is often given as the reason for poor economies in places like Nigeria. I would be the first to admit the devastating effect of corruption by unaccountable and often undemocratic leaders. However, most of the stolen funds are stashed away in foreign banks. Returning the money to Nigeria is the appropriate solution, instead of punishing the majority of the population who spend years of their life in poverty.

The Nigerian situation is not unique almost 90 countries have worked with the IMF for over a decade. It is strange that the IMF finds it hard to point to even a handful of success stories. In most cases, as Rudiger Dornbusch of the Massachusetts Institute of Technology, says, structural adjustment caused developing economies to "fall into a hole". Low investment reduced spending and low output created a vicious cycle of decline and stagnation, rather than one of growth, rising employment and rising investment. The World Bank IMF theory had backfired.

By contrast, many observers noticed that the Chinese economy grew by 7.8% last year, while the rest of the region fell deep into recession. Ironically, China is now helping to save the globalisers from themselves. It has kept its fixed exchange rate, rather than devaluing to get a larger share of shrinking regional export markets.

Instead of pursuing a beggar thy neighbour strategy, China has shifted resources to domestic production. The Government is spending $200 billion on public works this year. Fortunately, China has more autonomy to pursue rational policies than most developing countries: its currency is not freely convertible, its financial system is domestically owned and controlled by the State and there is little foreign ownership of equities. And it does not have to take orders from the IMF.

Since its policies have failed the IMF is now trying hard to sell itself as a development agency committed to fighting poverty but, predictably, not everyone is buying.

"When the IMF speaks of poverty relief it's like telling someone who is beating their wife, 'We're going to provide transport for your wife to the hospital',", says Alejandro Bendana, president of Nicaragua's Centre for International Studies.

The IMF says it is giving its embattled Enhanced Structural Adjustment Facility (ESAF) a new name—the Poverty Reduction and Growth Facility in an effort to put social concerns at the centre of its efforts to restructure impoverished economies while relieving their debts.

However, the IMF is not trying to change its policy but is adding conditions to its list of demands on nations in debt. The IMF is also stressing the need to increase trade to boost economic growth in poor countries.

" But if we continue with the existing international division of labour, where we in Africa are reduced to producing what we do not consume and consuming what we do not produce, we are going to get nowhere," says Odour Ong'wen of EcoNews Africa, a Kenya based non governmental organisation tracking trade, finance and environmental issues.

Over 40 years ago most economists knew the State had a vital role to play in economic development and that unregulated markets alone would polarise the distribution of income and wealth and could lead to panics, recessions and depressions. They also knew that industrialisation and economic development required some protection from international market forces as well as planning and that the later any country arrived on the scene, the more state intervention it would need.

There are many paths to economic development and the first pre condition for helping the poor is to break the foreign stranglehold on their governments. This is where the anti globalisation protesters in Prague can make a difference. Since the success of the anti globalisation protesters in Seattle last year, a mass movement for worldwide economic democracy and justice has been taking shape. It has the potential to be as powerful as the anti apartheid movement in the 1980s and help the world in its struggle against economic colonialism and the poverty that comes with it.

26th September 2000

*   *   *

Too many casualties when
we trade democracy for profit to get fiscally fit

IN the last few days, globalisation and market forces, the much-hyped panacea of world economics, have gone awry. Bloodshed in the Middle East, volatility in oil prices, the unending troubles of the European single currency, euro induced inflation at home and falling corporate profits in Europe for powerful multinationals have unsettled the stock markets and ordinary consumers on both sides of the Atlantic. The continuing influence of local circumstances and politics on the precarious global economy is stronger than ever.

In the 1990s globalisation was shamelessly hyped for the good fortune it would bring. Ethnic hatreds would melt away as the Internet and McDonald's hamburger stalls spread worldwide. Expanding free markets would cure the world's ills. Many, such as US President Bill Clinton, preached the doctrine of interdependence. In that Promised Land, it was not terribly important who was in charge. The markets were.

Yet on a daily basis we are confronted with a failure to consolidate economic and political gains from the new single currency, the euro. Foreign investment and large-scale exports are key factors in upholding the economic boom. On this basis Ireland's entry into the euro zone was a positive move and Irish exporters have seen their profits grow. However, the fact that our major trading partner, Britain, avoided the euro means that with so many British imports, we are continually importing inflation.

The trouble with the euro is that it has allowed European companies and individuals to get large amounts of capital and spend that money not in Europe but in the United States. Europeans invested $200 billion more in US companies and assets during the past year than Americans put into Europe in direct investment. This is in part globalisation working, as it should. European businessmen have understood that the fastest and surest way to invest in Asia often is to buy American companies that do business there, or to buy shares in the US owned General Electric (GE) company for example and let GE decide how to manage global profits and risk.

But fear as well as greed seems to be motivating the capital flight. The euro has drifted downward from its launch level of $1.17 to about 84 cents. A halfhearted monetary intervention by the Group of Seven finance ministers in September had no lasting effect. Last week, president of the European Central Bank, Wim Duisenberg, was vilified for ruling out further central bank intervention to prop up the ailing currency. By appearing to support intervention that previously failed to stabilise the euro, the financial wizards have inadvertently revealed that they are not in control of the global economy.

Perhaps, we need to think again. Globalisation needs to be replaced by localisation protecting and rebuilding local economies. Long distance trade would be gradually reduced to supplying what could not come from within one country or region. Trade would be conducted under rules that give preference to goods supplied in a way that benefits workers, the local community and the environment. The global flow of technology and information would be encouraged only when and where it could strengthen local economies.

This does not mean a return to overpowering state control. But new rules would have to be enacted to stop imported goods and services that could be produced locally. Industries will have to be put in the local community if they are to win permission to sell in it.

Today's global casino consists of traders gambling on minute market fluctuations. In 1980, the daily average of foreign trading was $80 billion. Today, more than $1,500 billion flows daily across international borders. Up to 90% of transactions are speculative (based on movements in currency and interest rates) rather than productive. Democratic control over such capital is the key to providing the money for governments and communities to rebuild. In addition to tax on international capital transactions to curb currency speculators, broader re regulation of finance capital will be required. This would include controls on capital flows, taxes on short term speculative transactions, tightening of easy credit that allows speculators to multiply the size of their bets way beyond the cash required to cover them. A widespread and coordinated attack on corporate tax evasion, including offshore banking centres, is also essential. The markets would immediately punish any country proposing such controls on its own. However, a regional grouping of powerful states such as the European Union would be a secure and lucrative enough market to ensure that those who control money would not dare leave the safety and security afforded by such a bloc. This pattern would then be attempted globally.

Politically, the 20th century was a battle between left and right. In the 21st century the contest will pit localists against those struggling to manage globalisation. The former will seek control over the local economy; the latter will continue to see globalisation as inevitable as gravity. Their role will be to attempt to make it a better balance for all of us. **24th October 2000**

*   *   *

Eradicating Malaria from Africa

Surely human lives are a very high price to pay for environmental protection?

Naturally, there is always a risk that Africa's legendary creatures; the lion, the elephant, the snake or the rhinoceros might be hazardous to human health. But the biggest danger to Africans is one of the world's tiniest creatures: the mosquito. This insect transmits malaria, a brutal and debilitating disease that kills 2.7 million people every year. As one expert puts it, that's like crashing seven jumbo passenger planes every day.

The good news is that in the fight against malaria we have a weapon that is cheap, easy to use and highly effective. The bad news is that it's DDT, a substance banned in much of the developed world, and, if environmentalists get their way, to be outlawed everywhere before long.

Widely used as an agricultural pesticide after World War II, DDT came to be seen as an agent of ecological destruction in the late '60s. It was banned in the US in 1972 (and later in 33 other western countries) because of evidence that it was helping wipe out the peregrine falcon, the bald eagle and other birds. It was one of the toxic substances cited by Rachel Carson in her landmark 1962 book Silent Spring, which trumpeted the dangers of various pesticides and helped generate the new movement known as environmentalism.

Wealthy, healthy nations in Europe and North America suffered no real penalty from giving up DDT. But, in recent years, it's become clear that many of the world's poorest countries are paying a heavy price for following that course not only in the loss of lives, but also in their economic prosperity.

For those people in tropical countries at risk from malaria, DDT offers by far the best hope of deliverance. Without sustained efforts to keep the disease at bay, these countries suffer from the dual hardships of a greatly depleted workforce and reduced productivity. Jeffrey Sachs, a development economist at Harvard University, estimates that sub Saharan Africa would be almost a third richer today had the disease been eradicated in 1965.

Using this pesticide may sound like a terrible idea to anyone who remembers it as the surest way to put species on the endangered list. But in the bad old days, DDT was sprayed in huge volumes on fields of crops to kill insects. Nobody proposes to do that today. What public health experts endorse is spraying small amounts on the indoor walls of homes in malarial zones.

Donald Roberts, a tropical disease specialist at Uniformed Services University of Health Sciences in Bethesda, (US), says that, in studies, when they have sprayed two houses, one with DDT and one with a more toxic pesticide, mosquitoes have readily entered the latter while staying away from the one with DDT. Since mosquitoes are most active at night, when people are indoors, DDT sharply reduces the transmission of malaria.

The widespread use of DDT in the '50s and '60s all but eliminated malaria in several developing countries and saved an estimated 500m lives by 1970. Since then, the use of the stuff has shrunk. Of the roughly 100 countries where malaria is endemic, only 23 now employ DDT to fight the disease. And that is frequently the fault of aid donors who help to finance the battle against malaria.

In the early 1990s, for example, the United States Agency for International Development stopped the governments of Bolivia and Belize from using DDT. In Madagascar, the United Nations Development Programme tried to persuade the government to replace DDT with Propoxur, a less effective pesticide. To its credit, Madagascar refused.

In Mozambique, NORAD, the Norwegian development agency, and SIDA, its Swedish counterpart, said that they could not support the use of DDT as it was banned in their own countries. That the problems of a desperately poor malarial country in Africa were somewhat different from those of wealthy, non malarial Scandinavia seems not to have occurred to them.

When DDT spraying stops, malarial transmissions explode. South Africa stopped spraying in 1996. Its caseload subsequently rose by 150%. It recently started spraying again, and the disease is retreating. In Mozambique, infection rates are 20 40 times higher than in neighbouring Swaziland, which has never stopped using DDT. During the 1990s, countries like Brazil and Peru saw their malaria rates soar after stopping the use of DDT. Ecuador expanded its DDT spraying during that period and cut its infection rate by 60%.

Environmental groups that want a worldwide ban, notably the World Wildlife Fund, say countries with a problem should use other pesticides. But that's like saying firemen should fight blazes with anything but water. Roberts and other public health experts say nothing is as effective as DDT.

The alternatives are not only inferior but more expensive—a critical consideration for poor countries with modest healthcare budgets.

The risks of a selective, small-scale use of DDT are nothing compared to the risks of not using it. Though the chemical's residues do show up in the human body, it's not clear they do any harm. Though it may disrupt reproduction in some animals, the amounts that would be used in indoor spraying would have only a minimal effect.

Human lives have to take priority over wildlife. If grizzly bears or wolves were eating hundreds or thousands of Europeans or Americans every year, no one would offer them protection. Malaria kills millions. We can only be sanguine about the death toll because we are not the ones paying it.

In a draft United Nations treaty recently approved by representatives of 120 countries, a proposal to set a 2007 deadline for a global ban was dropped. But countries that insist on spraying DDT will be subject to monitoring.

The treaty drafted in Johannesburg, due to be signed in May, is a welcome antidote to the DDT nonsense. But it is still far from ideal. Countries that use DDT for malaria control will be forced to record and report how much they use, how they use it and where they get it from. This may not sound onerous, but in places such as Mozambique, where the annual budget for fighting malaria is less than 30 cents a person, any additional bureaucracy could prove to be a big drain on resources. Concern for the environment is generally an admirable thing. Obsession, at the cost of human lives, is of more questionable value. **9th January 2001**

*   *   *

Success at the Olympics is in the hands of those who hold the most cash

Despite the lofty ideals that inspire the Olympic Games and the riveting razzmatazz of the extravagant opening ceremony in Sydney last Friday, it is wishful and romantic thinking to assume the sporting jamboree is a level playing pitch for athletes from economically disadvantaged countries. In truth, it has been and it remains an expensive jamboree where only those who can afford to send their best, play to win.

Of course, there will be notable exceptions, but by and large the role of the impoverished will be that they are pleased merely to be at the party. The reality is that participation and success in the modern Olympics goes to the wealthy, the powerful, the full time professional.

Indeed, the concept of amateur sports and the altruistic sporting passion that comes with it, may be true for Gaelic games, but is a barely concealed fiction at the modern Olympics. Indeed, far from bearing any genuine resemblance to the ancient Greek games (apart from being thankfully, bloodless) it is actually closer to the Roman gladiator contests—namely a contest between unequals.

In Sydney, as elsewhere, the playing field is far from level. As a senior official with one African team, who declined to be named, said: "There is a lot of talk about drug cheats. But what about the cash cheats? Rich nations can buy success. If you want more medals, just inject more cash".

That may be a bit harsh but consider the contrasts on show: top sprinters such as American Michael Johnson arriving with multimillion dollar shoe deals with Nike, while East Timorese marathon runner Aguida Amaral was still seeking a pair of shoes as recently as June.

While footballers like Australian Mark Viduka who is reported to earn about £30,000 a week must weigh up whether he can afford not to participate, some of the world's poorest nations such as Burkina Faso (four athletes), Sierra Leone (eight) and Congo (five) question whether they can afford to come to the games at all.

Being a national Olympic hero is a luxury for poorer countries, such as India, for instance. Even before the recent flooding in the north of the country left hundreds of thousands homeless, authorities decided that tackling chronic, large scale poverty was more important than playing sport. Despite its proud sporting tradition, India has sent only 72 athletes and 47 officials to Sydney its largest team but still relatively small for a nation of more than 1 billion.

In an obvious but inadequate gesture to bridge the gap between the rich and poor nations, the International Olympic Committee established, for the first time ever, the Sydney 2000 Olympic Solidarity scholarships. This worldwide programme makes an award available to help promising athletes who lack the cash or the coaching to compete. In all, scholarships were awarded to 150 athletes presently competing in Sydney a drop in the ocean, when you consider that the total number of athletes in this year' s game is 11,000.

It could of course be argued that funding would be better invested in the provision of local sport facilities in the disadvantaged countries where it would be of huge benefit to thousands.

A case in point is that of Paula Barila Bolopa, a swimmer from the Republic of Equatorial Guinea in West Africa. For Balopa, a 50 metre freestyle swimmer, the dream of a gold medal is a distant one. In her hometown Malabo there is no Olympic size pool so Bolopa trains twice a week in a 20-metre pool in a local hotel. At times she cannot use it because there are too many hotel guests. During weekends she swims in the sea, watched over by her trainer and team coach, Bernardo Elonga Moliko.

The Equatorial Guinea team members have no uniforms and this is worth remembering when Bolopa takes to the pool next week for her first heat in the 50 metres freestyle. Such are the disadvantaged and distractions, which face some competitors.

She does not have one of the streamlined swimsuits specially designed for speed that will be used at the games by the richest athletes courtesy of their multi million pound sponsors.

Bolopa' s best time for 50 metres is about 30 seconds. The current gold medalist, Amy van Dyke, of the US, won in 1996 in 24.87 seconds. "I don't think anybody will be interested in giving me a suit but there is no doubt that it would help me become faster," said Bolopa. "Athletes like me are already at a disadvantage before the event begins, how can I compete with someone who has the best equipment and coaching?"

After the medals have been won at the Sydney Games, the IOC will have to give some serious consideration to restructuring the competition to make it more meaningful for all participants.

Aside from the need to invest in sports facilities in poorer countries, it might be an idea to extend representation at the Olympics to individual continents, rather than countries. This would mean, hopefully, that as a result of continental representation, there would be a reduced competitive pool at the final stages and a less defensive attitude from national sporting bodies when their sporting icons are caught out in drugs testing scandals.

We could only hope also that Olympian feats would become more credible and rewarding for the honest and sometimes poorer athletes.

Presently, the range of individual events at the Olympic games is far bigger than what is necessary; there are certainly many events that have crept into the Olympic pantheon that do not deserve to be there. Basketball is a prime example not because it is a team sport, however. The reason why basketball should be omitted is precisely the reason why it was admitted: to use the pulling power of US basketball stars to attract North American television audiences. This, of course, is another example of how commercialism has tainted the ideals that inspire the Games.

The Olympics Games therefore ought to be an event primarily for sports that are not already dominated by highly paid professionals. They ought to be about the spreading of Olympic glory around the world, not its ever-greater concentration in the same affluent hands. **19th September 2000**

*   *   *

Airlines' profit is our loss when safety takes back seat

With all the low cost plane fares on offer, it was reassuring to hear last week that the Australian government has ordered an inquiry into the life threatening economy class syndrome.

The following day the British government pledged to carry out research into the blood clots caused by cramped conditions on long haul flights and force changes if necessary. Given the number of transatlantic flights every day, it is astonishing that we have heard nothing from our own Government.

Until last October few airline passengers worried about blood clots. Then a 28-year-old Welsh woman, fitness fanatic Emma Christoffersen, stepped off a plane at Heathrow Airport after a 12,000 mile journey from Australia and collapsed and died. An autopsy attributed her death to a pulmonary embolism. In other words a blood clot had lodged in her lung.

The likely cause of the clot was her restricted movement in cramped seating during the long trip.

Since then economy class syndrome has drawn a lot of attention.

Two weeks ago a hospital near Heathrow Airport reported that at least 30 people had died over the last three years after long flights. That's the toll at just one hospital near one airport.

Across the Atlantic, some aviation experts estimate that several hundred economy class syndrome deaths occur in the United States every year.

No one is really sure, though, because the symptoms of a clot, which can include swelling and cramping, vary and are often mistaken for something else.

In many cases, passengers who develop clots may not seek medical treatment until days after their flight, lessening the chance that a connection can be made between their complaint and recent air travel.

Research to be published in the British Medical Journal reveals that one tenth of blood clots treated at one London hospital were caused by restricted movement on flights. Nationally, these figures would point to 3,000 cases a year and 300 deaths.

Pilots and aircrew have also been victims of economy class syndrome. One pilot, writing on the Professional Pilots' website, said: "I can confirm that air crew have in the past and still do, suffer from Deep Vain Thrombosis. I suffered a pulmonary embolism at the age of 37. Recently a colleague suffered the same fate and luckily he survived as I did. I sincerely hope no one suffers the same fate, but unfortunately it does happen."

To reduce the risks, doctors recommend that passengers sit on the aisle or near a bulkhead to increase legroom, drink plenty of water and avoid alcohol on flights to prevent dehydration.

Walking around once an hour or at least doing foot and leg stretches will also help. The trouble with this advice is obvious: there are a limited number of aisle and bulkhead seats and strolling around crowded planes is a bit of a challenge.

The most common sense solution of all gets little mention. Note that the clotting problem isn't described as first class syndrome. It's called economy class syndrome because of the limited space between the seats where most passengers sit. Removing a few rows of seats, as some airlines on some routes are already doing, would certainly allow for greater movement, presumably lowering the risk of Deep Vein Thrombosis.

Removing seats does reduce airline profits, but as more evidence of clotting turns up we can only hope the airlines will realise the additional cost is worth it.

Already, lawsuits are being taken in Australia. The airlines understand the health risk, which is why some give written warnings to passengers or videos encouraging stretching. But these are really no substitutes for room to move.

Proof that long periods stuck in cramped airline seats might be a health risk has commercial implications for airlines. Companies would have to enlarge seat spaces and increase overhead storage capacity to prevent baggage being stowed underneath seats, thus restricting leg movement. Beds would be even better.

Passenger payloads per flight would decline, of course, forcing ticket prices up and reducing passenger numbers.

We need proper scientific evidence from long haul passengers and the research needs to be properly controlled. It can be up to a fortnight before the side effects of economy class syndrome are noticed.

Sadly, the poor response of airlines to a succession of deaths already gives serious grounds for concern. That no proper action is taken with some airlines even considering reducing seat spaces even further demonstrates that the pursuit of profit and shareholder value now ranks far too highly as a corporate objective. Health and safety seems less of a priority.

With more low cost airlines targeting Dublin Airport in their expansion plans for this year, this is not a time for government inactivity while lives are at risk.

The Government should look into this life threatening issue with a view to protecting the public interest, as matter of urgency.

One task often easily dismissed as bureaucratic and costly is to make sure that public interests are addressed by ensuring that lower costs are not achieved at the expense of public health and safety concerns. **23rd January 2001**

*   *   *

It's a bigger tragedy when we aid nature on her trail of destruction

It is often said that humans are the biggest threat to the environment. True. But it is also true that the biggest threat to us is the environment. Last week's earthquake in India has shown, like hurricanes and droughts before it, that nature is a ruthless mass killer.

Of all the towns rocked by the catastrophic earthquake in India, Bhachau has been the most devastated. Before last week 25,000 people lived there. Rescuers say they can find only 5,000. The rest have simply vanished and 90% of the area has been wiped out.

Charles Darwin would have told you that you do not need earthquakes or hurricanes to understand that mass killing is an integral part of the environment. In your back garden various rival grasses and weeds; insects and worms are battling for space and survival. If the temperature goes up a couple of degrees it helps some species overcome others. If humidity rises marginally that helps some survive while others perish. A deadly war to the death is going on under your very eyes, under cover of what looks like a peaceful green lawn. Only the fittest survive.

Last week there was a big oil spill in the Galapagos Islands, a place that helped Darwin formulate his theory of evolution. Environmentalists warned of the threat oil spill posed to many unique species in the Galapagos Islands. Situated far off the coast of South America, the sheer isolation of the islands has helped its species evolve in unique ways. The original animals flew or swam from the mainland to the islands, but developed over the millennia to produce the world's only marine iguanas, land iguanas, unique giant tortoises and mocking birds. An ecological paradise, it attracts thousands of tourists.

Ecuador's Government wisely limits the number of tourists per year, to reduce the strain on the environment.

Ironically, nature could wreak far more havoc on the animals than tourists. The cold Humboldt Current wells up and brings a huge amount of plankton and other marine food to the sea around the islands. This supports large colonies of sea lions, pelicans and other fish eating birds. The coldness of the current also reduces rainfall.

The islands are not green at all and land based creatures thrive less than marine ones. Land iguanas, giant tortoises and mocking birds are thin on the ground.

But once in a while along comes El Nino, producing a change of ocean currents. Around the islands, the warm Panama Current replaces the cold Humboldt Current. This has much less plankton and marine food and so suddenly the sea lions and fish eating birds find that there is not enough to eat. It is estimated that 80% of the sea lions in Galapagos died last year when El Nino arrived.

Nature's selection was ruthless. Those who died were the very young or old, the sick, the crippled. There was no mercy for the weak. Only the fittest survived. Nature is elitist; it favours the strong over the weak and handicapped.

But the warm current brought by El Nino last year also brought more rainfall and this helped all land species on the islands to strengthen. Vegetation flourished, there was more water and biomass for all land based creatures and their population increased. Mocking birds suddenly seemed to be everywhere.

But nature is capricious. El Nino typically lasts only one year. After killed thousands of animals, it sneaks away and the cold current returns. This is a blessing for the sea lions and pelicans whose population once again begins to soar. But the decline in rainfall means suddenly there is not enough water or biomass on land to support the population explosion caused by El Nino. Land creatures begin to die in droves. That is nature' s way of creating an ecological balance.

I have always been amused by the romantic pastoralist notion that nature provides enough for everybody's need, but not for everybody's greed. This implies that nature is bountiful while man is a greedy consumer. Try telling that to the creatures on the Galapagos Islands. Try telling it to those killed by the Gujarat earthquake or Orissa cyclone.

Despite all nature's glories, many have witnessed its cruelty. It uses mass starvation for social engineering, systematically killing the weakest and letting only the strongest survive.

While debunking ecological romanticism, one must not debunk ecology wholesale, or condone our environmental damage. The fact that nature is a mass killer does not mean we should add to its destruction.

To the ravages of earthquakes and hurricanes, El Ninos and droughts, we should not add the ravages of soil and water degradation.

In Gujurat local developers who ignored building safety codes and the local authorities that permitted such poor construction contributed to the death of hundreds of victims.

Our aim must be to provide a more secure environment where we are all less at risk. We can do nothing to stop earthquakes and hurricanes, but we can reduce environmental degradation. **30th January 2001**

*   *   *

Time for a Marshall Plan for Africa?

Perhaps the devastation that Africa endures today is seen as incomparable to that faced by Europe after the Second World War. The effect is the same. A continent that is bankrupt and unable to repay crippling debts.

Why is the world not willing today to consider a Marshall Plan for Africa? Can it be because the affinity of a common origin is lacking or is it because nobody in the proper position is confronting the world with the parallels between a prostrate Europe in 1947 and a prostrate Africa in 2000?

It is time to canvass for a similar rescue package for Africa. What was the Marshall Plan?

A coordinated effort by the U.S. and many nations of Europe to foster European economic recovery after WORLD WAR II. First urged (June 5, 1947) by U.S. Sec. of State George C. MARSHALL, the program was administered by the Economic Cooperation Administration (ECA) and from 1948 to 1951 dispensed more than $12 billion in American aid.

The following extracts from General Marshall's original speech are as relevant in Africa today as they were in Europe in 1947:

1. "The remedy lies in breaking the vicious circle and restoring the confidence of the [European] people in the economic future of their own countries and of Europe as a whole."

2. " Aside from the demoralizing effect on the world at large and the possibilities of disturbances arising as a result of the desperation of the people concerned, the consequences to the economy of the United States should be apparent to all. It is logical that the United States should do whatever it is able to do to assist in the return of normal economic health in the world, without which there can be no political stability and no assured peace. Our policy is directed not against any country or doctrine but against hunger, poverty, desperation and chaos. Its purpose should be the revival of a working economy in the world so as to permit the emergence of political and social conditions in which free institutions can exist. Such assistance, I am convinced, must not be on a piecemeal basis as various crises develop. Any assistance that this Government may render in the future should provide a cure rather than a mere palliative."

3. "Furthermore, the people of this country are distant from the troubled areas of the earth and it is hard for them to comprehend the plight and consequent reactions of the long-suffering peoples, and the effect of those reactions on their governments in connection with our efforts to promote peace in the world".

4. "The truth of the matter is that Europe's requirements for the next three or four years of foreign food and other essential products—principally from America—are so much greater than her present ability to pay that she must have substantial additional help or face economic, social, and political deterioration of a very grave character".

5. "Aside from the demoralizing effect on the world at large and the possibilities of disturbances arising as a result of the desperation of the people concerned, the consequences to the economy of the United States should be apparent to all. It is logical that the United States should do whatever it is able to do to assist in the return of normal economic health in the world, without which there can be no political stability and no assured peace". **April 24 2000**

LIFE IN A BOOMING ECONOMY —THE IRISH CELTIC TIGER

This is undeniably the golden age of Ireland's economic boom. Speaking to the Social Partners last week, Tanaiste Mary Harney declared that the present Government was "awash with funds". The Revenue Commissioners collected almost £24bn in tax receipts last year and consumers are spending like there is no tomorrow. So does everyone benefit? Not likely. The losers are very young, the elderly and the vulnerable. So much for the benefits of the Celtic Tiger.

Consumers have never had it so good. The value of goods bought by Irish shoppers was a staggering 20 percent more during the month of May than the same month last year an increase described by the Central Statistics Office as "huge". Apparently, cuts in taxes and falling unemployment have encouraged a strong feel-good sentiment among consumers, who have reacted by spending heavily in department stores on electrical goods and clothing. But how does the average family unit fare in this economy? As labour shortages continue to occur in virtually every major sector of the economy, one positive effect are the unprecedented opportunities for married women. While the additional family income is a great boost, the issue of childcare continues to defy any solution. From all accounts, the cost of childcare in Ireland is one of the highest in the EU.

More disturbing is an unpublished report prepared by the ESRI that suggests almost one child in every four is living in a household dependent on a means-tested social welfare benefit for at least some of its income. It's not only children who are relying on means-tested social welfare benefits. At the end of December last, a total of 384,000 adults were in receipt of a means tested benefit and they were also getting payments in respect of 82,000 adult dependants. So there are a total of 466,000 adults on means-tested benefits. That's 12.5 per cent of the population i.e. one person in eight. A Eurostat report showed the Government's output on social welfare in the 1990s has steadily dropped, leaving Ireland as the lowest spender on people in need in the EU.

Without the benefits of tax breaks and cuts, those registered unemployed are now worse off than they were before last year's Budget. The value of unemployment assistance, the minimum social welfare payment, has fallen by 26pence this year due to the impact of inflation. Inflation has reduced the value of last year's dole by £4.26, while the Department of Social Welfare increase for this year was set at £4.00. Although inflation at 5.5percent has also wiped out the Programme for Prosperity and Fairness (PPF) wages increases for most workers, at least they have the additional benefit of tax cuts, which boost their spending power by between 4 percent and 8 percent.

Affluence is supposedly the major result of the Tiger economy; acquisition is a byproduct of affluence. Acquisition for it's own sake is partly to blame for the housing crisis which now exists, particularly in urban areas, where despite the recent tweaking by Government on the recommendation of the Bacon report, many young couples remain effectively priced out of the Property market. 1998 estimates for those priced out of the property market were in the region of 20,000 for that year alone.

By any gauge, the most outstanding achievement of the Celtic Tiger has been the rapid erosion of the bane of unemployment and the phenomenal creation of new jobs, which along with the impressive Irish economic growth rates are the envy of the entire world. However there is also less job security. While the young are not particularly bothered by the talk of lifetime education and continuous training, others look back to the stability of old jobs with understandable nostalgia. In the Software industry (where I work) it is not unusual to hear of well paid permanent jobs being turned down, because some IT Professionals do not want to miss out on more lucrative but transient opportunities by being be tied down. It is foreseeable that in the near future with family commitments, the same IT Professionals may take a more favourable view of the "steady" job alternative especially with it's access to an occupational pension. Despite all the opportunities offered by new technology in the Celtic Tiger, it also appears undeniable that people are working harder, and for longer hours. "Globalisation" is usually blamed as the Celtic Tiger battles for new investments and invariably jobs with Asian Tigers where wages and costs are often lower.

In many ways, the Catholic Church is undoubtedly one of the biggest losers of the advent of the Celtic Tiger. There has always been an inverse relationship between affluence and religious practice; the decline in church attendance may well be more related to the indifference of affluence than to conscientious disillusionment with the institution itself. The divorce referendum of 1995 was the church's Waterloo in the "moral civil war" as the Celtic Tiger began to roar ever louder. With the loss of previous battles such as liberalisation of contraceptive sales, the decriminalisation of homosexuality in 1993, and the loosening of the prohibition on abortion as a result of the X-case in 1992, the moral civil war was always going to be lost. Furthermore following Casey's resignation in May 1992 and the tide of sex scandals followed, Bishops were soon in no position to lecture on morality as their priests trooped in and out of court on paedophilia charges.

The relative loss of spirituality in the Celtic Tiger has come at a cost; if religion acted as an influence for good in controlling impulsive and self-destructive behaviours then its absence has created a vacuum that has to be filled. There is fear of a deeper malaise of crass materialism damaging the national character, replacing the much admired Irish traditional generosity and sympathy for the underdog. Remarkably, Simon, the voluntary service for the homeless, has to rely on volunteers from overseas to run its projects. Last Monday 31st July, Simon's national director Conall Mac Riocaird indicated that up to 80 percent of the full-time volunteers who work with the Simon Community are recruited from abroad, as Irish charity workers become increasingly difficult to find. About four years ago, 80 percent of volunteers were Irish. Sadly, it seems the drive for economic success is eroding the tradition of altruism among young people.

Many will remember the Donnelly US visas issued in 1992 to 1994, it is a measure of the success of Celtic Tiger today that Irish emigrants are returning by the tens of thousands on an annual basis. Naturally such economic success attracts foreign citizens; therefore it is now usual to find thousands of American expatriates and executives working in many parts of Ireland without any problem whatsoever. By contrast, the apparent intolerance in some quarters towards Refugees and Asylum seekers has received wide coverage by the media. Unfortunately, this has tended not only to overshadow the selfless and commendable work of many Irish volunteers working in Asylum support groups all over the country but it has also challenged the pre-Celtic Tiger view, that "racism" (or more accurately xenophobia) is very negligible in this country. Disturbingly, very recent reports suggest some foreign students especially from Spain appear to be experiencing similar intolerance

With a shadow of doubt, the rise of the Celtic Tiger is a great source of pride and self-confidence, much of which is well deserved; the arrival of each and every returning Irish emigrant, in effect reverses the legacy of the Great Famine and that is a credit. On the debit side of the balance sheet, we must be carefully not to let the affluence of the Celtic Tiger reverse the caring spirit of the kind people of this great nation. **August 1st 2000**

*   *   *

Small savers paying dearly as big banks cut their costs

As we enter the age of billion pound per year bank profits, it might be reasonable to ask if ordinary bank customers are sharing the benefits of these bonuses. Does the argument that banks are an ordinary commercial venture absolve them from social responsibility to the customer they claim to serve?

Last Friday, a top level Government banking review group confirmed what many of us had long suspected i.e. the country's banking sector is the most profitable in Europe. The group's report indicated that, during the '90s, Irish banks had a higher return on assets than any other EU country.

It is a fact of modern life that many of us have absolutely no choice about whether we use the bank or not. Many workers receive their salary as a lodged payment, made directly into a named bank account by employers reluctant to pay their staff through other channels. While acknowledging that banks have a commercial requirement to make profit, there is an increasing awareness that banks also have a social responsibility to their customers and the community they serve.

Banking with a social and ethical conscience is not as utopian as it initially sounds; there are examples in other countries. The UK based Co-operative Bank runs its banking services on ethical principles. More recently, in response to the recent closure of rural branches of the Barclays bank, the British Government has announced its intention to set up a universal bank in post offices to provide services to the "financially excluded". In Australia, there are all in one bank accounts designed to minimise customers' interest payments by mixing salaries, mortgages, savings and credit cards.

Here, the credit union movement is one of our unsung treasures, with half of the population belonging to a credit union. Already substantial areas of rural Ireland use the credit union system as a major banking method not just because it avoids problems or deals with crises, but because it is socially constructive and personally positive. A social investment of this sort creates people who have an investment in co-operation whilst recognising and nurturing self-reliance at the same time. It's an investment towards a society of people who have a stake in the health of their environment and local economy.

Unfortunately, it appears that more persuasion is required if the Minister for Finance is to develop a more favourable attitude to resolving the outstanding issue regarding his attempts to impose higher DIRT taxation on savings held in credit unions. However, with the prospect of banks paying even less corporation tax within the next three years, the Minister's argument for imposing higher DIRT taxes on savings held in the more socially productive credit unions has become a much less tenable one. Indeed, the provision of incentives to invest in credit unions is quite sensible as banks cut back on branches.

Last week, the AIB announced a record pre tax half-year profit of £480 million, making it the first Irish company with a realistic possibility of earning £1 billion profit in one calendar year. Calculated on a daily basis, the AlB's record half-year earnings represent a profit of £2.64m a day the equivalent of its entire one-year's profit 30 years ago. Despite making pre tax profits of £724.5 million, the Bank of Ireland last week informed its staff in five Dublin branches that they will be closed down in December, in the opening move of a cost cutting plan which could involve the closure of up to 20% of its outlets. Similarly, First Active announced a cost cutting programme last year and subsequently closed 25 branches at a cost of £26 million.

While the AIB does not have a scheme for reducing its number of outlets, it recently announced the phasing out of its swipe cash lodgements facility for credit cards in AIB branches, in a bid to transfer such services to its telephone banking division. Only time will tell if other banking services at AIB branches will be phased out.

With the banks making so much money, it is difficult to see how they can justify their cost cutting and service reduction moves. In such circumstances, public cynicism is not unexpected. A recent TV programme began with the following introduction: "Banks are making billions. And they want more. They're squeezing out the customers who don't make them money."

As the banks continue to cut back on unprofitable outlets and switch over to electronic banking, hapless customers are left with few real substitutes. For many (especially in isolated rural towns and villages) credit unions may be the only real alternative.

It is questionable whether credit unions will ever entirely fill the gap left by bank branch closures. But they would like to be seen as mainstream forms of financial provision, rather than a last resort for the poor. As mutual organisations, where profit is not the main criteria for success, the credit unions should have a head start over banks in becoming viable in areas where the big financial institutions have failed.

Perhaps the time has come for the Government to redress the balance by reviewing restrictions on credit unions. The self-help banking movement is a relatively small one with a limited range of services.

Credit unions do not have the power to offer cash machine services, overdrafts or mortgages. But they have big ambitions and hope they may eventually be able to offer a much wider range of services.

As banks scale down their traditional mode of service delivery in favour of more profitable internet and telephone banking, it may be worthwhile for Government and the big banks to look into the possibility of banks working in co operation with credit unions to extend basic current accounts to low income earners where access to regular bank branches do not exist.

The Ulster Bank's parent company announced its intention to enter into similar arrangements in Britain last week. If on the other hand, banks are unwilling to extend such co-operation to credit unions, another option could be windfall taxes on huge banking profits.

Proceeds from this tax could help the customers banks no longer consider worthwhile. **August 8th 2000**

*   *   *

Siege mentality on shooting inquiry won't heal the wound

The rationale of an unarmed police force was never more keenly demonstrated than in the bloody aftermath of the 25-hour armed siege at Abbeylara, Co Longford, last April.

Anyone with experience of policing in other countries or across the border cannot fail to admire the long tradition of an unarmed police force in this country. Uniformed members of the gardaí do not carry firearms. The first Garda [*Police*] Commissioner, Michael Staines, said: "The Garda Síochána will achieve success not by force of arms but by its moral authority as servants of the people."

What does an unarmed police force need to do in order to maintain its moral authority and public confidence? Police transparency and accountability are fundamental for starters.

Seldom has an event sparked such public concern as the manner in which the gardaí handled the siege where John Carthy was shot dead outside his home.

The delay in the publication of the report of the internal garda inquiry and the latest decision by the DPP not to prosecute any of the officers involved in the fatal shooting will only further damage public confidence in the gardaí's handling of this case and, importantly, similar cases in the future.

Serious doubts remain about the appropriateness of the gardaí's response to the situation they faced in that quiet rural community. John Carthy (27) was shot four times in the legs and lower back after he pointed a shotgun at police and refused to put it down despite warnings. It remains unclear why it was necessary to shoot John Carthy in the back.

Reports indicate that garda regulations state officers should only fire their weapons "if they or members of the public are under direct threat from armed individuals". Was it not possible to disable Carthy with further shots to his legs?

It appears to be impossible to crack the shroud of secrecy that surrounds official policy in armed siege situations. The first two shots were directed at Carthy's legs, which indicate an intention only to disable him. One cannot help asking if there was a conscious decision to cause maximum injury with the fourth bullet that punctured his heart.

The most surprising aspect of this incident was the overwhelming force deployed by the gardaí. Why were Emergency Response Unit (ERU) marksmen and an additional 60 gardaí brought in to deal with a man armed only with a shotgun loaded with birdshot? The ERU officers were armed with Israeli-built Uzi submachine guns. In Britain the Heckler and Koch MP5 are the preferred options for police, including those in the North's RUC and London's Metropolitan Police. The Carthy family disputes garda claims that John forced his mother, Rose, out of her home. They are adamant that the dispute should have been sorted out peacefully.

The failure to use intermediaries trusted and requested by John Carthy, was a huge misjudgement on the part of the gardaí. What efforts were made by the gardaí to make contact with Michael Finucane, the solicitor with whom Carthy asked to speak? It took RTE''s Prime Time 25 seconds to get Finucane's mobile phone number from directory inquiries.

Last May, after a 10-hour siege, a serious hostage situation in the town of Hjelmeland, Norway, ended peacefully after one of Norway's best known criminal lawyers, Tor Erling Staff, went to meet the gunman as requested. The internal report on the John Carthy incident criticises the gardaí for their inability to locate Michael Finucane.

Criticism has also been directed at the gardaí for failing to set up a line of contact between John Carthy and his psychiatrist, David Shanley, who was at the scene. The report makes no special mention of this. In Britain, when a besieged person has a history of mental illness, as John Carthy had, the strategy of the police response changes immediately. A psychologist is called to the scene to provide the necessary psychological profile and assist in the negotiations. Armed officers at the scene are pulled back, so as not to create any further pressure for the individual. Indeed, armed response officers in Britain receive mental health training and are able to detect the relevant symptoms. No such allowances were made for John Carthy, a chain smoker, who was even denied his request for his favourite cigarettes. Months earlier however, a man involved in a siege in Co Kildare had been granted this fairly innocuous request. In addition to the inconsistencies and oversights made apparent by this incident was the failure of the FBI's top officers, including its deputy assistant director, to interview any of the witnesses.

Dealing with an emotionally disturbed person is one of the most difficult and dangerous tasks an officer might be forced to face. However, the gardaí are in a very privileged position, a position entrusted to them by the people of this country, which they should be prepared to submit for external review and scrutiny when the situation deems it necessary.

It is not acceptable that garda action and procedure were subject only to the investigations of other members of the force in the aftermath of Abbeylara. Since the events of that day were queried only by sources within the force itself, it comes as no surprise that many questions remain unanswered about the way this case was handled.

In an increasingly dangerous and violent world, the possibility of similar incidents happening in the future is more than likely. It would be naive to assume that this matter has been put to bed by the DPP's decision not to prosecute the officers involved.

The Government should set up an independent commission of inquiry to consider and investigate all aspects of this incident in a searching and transparent manner.

The inquiry's terms of reference should include recommendations that will give clear guidance for garda officers handling any similar future occurrence. These should ensure such incidents are settled in a humane manner. **August 15th 2000**

*　　　　　*　　　　　*

Despite progress the Net result is no one wants to risk their financial security

Last week's security breach of Eircom's Internet service by a hacker, who consequently had the ability to access the e mail accounts of over 30,000 customers, was another knock to the idealism and optimism that has greeted the advent of the Internet.

As the latest new technology to influence our lives, naturally it has generated more than its own fair share of hype. An intriguing question is finding out what has gone wrong with the Internet revolution which, given its immense potential, has arguably barely started. For starters, the Internet is not the first technology to have been hailed as a panacea and it will certainly not be the last.

Biotechnology is said to be the cure for world hunger. In the early years of the 20th century, aeroplanes were expected to end wars, by promoting international communication and (less credibly) by making armies obsolete, since they would be vulnerable to attack from the air. After the First World War had dispelled such notions, it was the turn of radio. "Nation shall speak peace unto nation," ran the fine motto of Britain's BBC World Service. Sadly, use of radio stations in war propaganda disproved the idea that radio was an intrinsically pacific force.

Hardly a day passes without us hearing about one dot.com or another. Frankly if you're not on-line (one of the industry's many buzzwords) you are more than likely to feel left out, or at least feel that you're missing out.

To be fair, the Internet does promote communication in ways that were previously unimaginable. Everything (or so the hype goes) is possible at the click of a button while surfing the web.

Daily on TV, radio, even in the print media, we are encouraged to run almost every aspect of our lives on the Internet. Banking, shopping, music (mp3s as the Internet jargon goes), chat rooms, sending cards; indeed anything seems possible on-line.

Unfortunately until a major fiasco happens like Eircom's debacle last week there is little mention of the risks we run, each time we use the Internet.

It's been argued that hackers like the one that wreaked havoc on Eircom are often not malicious. Hacking, said the spokeswoman for Eircom, was part of Internet life. It is easy to overlook how much personal information concerning net users, companies like Eircom (with a big presence on the Internet) store on their databases.

Beyond accessing news on the Internet, you can do very little without being asked for your name, marital status, earning power, address and invariably your credit card number. Accordingly, it is important for Internet users to know that such information is kept safe and secure from unscrupulous interlopers or hackers.

At the same time, we have to contend with the likelihood of receiving by e-mail, malicious computer programs, which could cause severe damage to our computers. A few of these programs, appropriately called viruses, have been known to cause companies world-wide huge financial losses worth millions of pounds.

Although you can guard against computer viruses by purchasing anti virus software, they are only useful if updated at least every month and they do not seem to be able to provide protection against future viruses.

Amazing as it may sound, despite all the hype about dot.coms and the benefits of e commerce, namely low costs, world-wide markets and so on, few companies are making real financial profit from the Internet. A string of fanciful dot.com companies failed in the States last year and Amazon, the number one bookshop on the web, despite its huge revenues has not made a penny of profit!

A case in point is the media business. Until recently, the Internet was seen as the ideal way of transacting media business in the 21st century. It was going to slash costs: media products, unlike most retail goods, can be delivered directly down wires, so the Internet would eliminate the need for factories and distribution networks.

It was going to boost revenues: previously inaccessible markets would become reachable and data collection would make advertising more valuable. And it was going to lower barriers to entry, generating a crop of healthy new companies. But the Internet has not lived up to these hopes. "To date," says Ted Leonsis, president of the Interactive Properties Group at AOL, "digital entertainment has been a failure."

There can be little doubt that the Internet changes many things. It has had a dramatic impact on the world of business. Firms can now link their systems directly to those of their suppliers and partners, can do business on-line around the clock, and can learn more than ever about their customers. Economies may be more productive as a result. For individuals, e-mail has emerged as the most important new form of personal communication since the invention of the telephone. Internet telephony making voice calls over the Internet is a big threat to the big phone companies who have been overcharging us for years for the luxury of making overseas calls.

Each new communication medium acts to open society further. The Post Office literally enabled a national government to communicate with its citizens. The telegraph made big business possible. The telephone allowed our families to remain in touch just as it enabled them to disperse and stop seeing each other. However everything comes at a cost; until the nagging security issues are tackled, public confidence in using the Internet for important transactions, which involve their finances, will plummet. The experience of Eircom has shown that it is an issue that has to be decisively tackled here in Ireland as well as other countries.

The heart of the problem appears to be anonymity on the web, which makes it difficult to trace expert hackers determined to show off their professional skills at everybody's expense. At the other end of the scale, we have a situation where the anonymity of the Internet makes it a convenient playing field for sexual perverts (and by extension the pornographic industry) with vulnerable and inexperienced youngsters being increasingly caught out.

Laws against crimes in cyberspace must be policed as vigorously as other laws are enforced. Perhaps it's time we borrowed a leaf from Sweden where there is a very stringent approach to Internet identification. **August 22nd 2000**

*   *   *

The violence of the small screen

Regrettably, violence is an enduring part of our existence. We are, of course, conditioned to a greater or lesser degree in our response to violence. Individual acts of violence can horrify us, and do so too often. Yet we continue to tolerate and accept violence as a norm, indeed sometimes it forms a perverse part of our multi-media television and film entertainment.

For many of us, last week's news that at least 1,400 victims of assault or unprovoked attacks were treated in Dublin hospitals for injuries in the first seven months of this year was a worrying and shocking development. More disturbing is the revelation by Victim Support that increasing numbers of victims of unprovoked attacks are young men aged between 17 and 25. Understandably, calls have been made for Parents of erring young men to be more accountable. The Deputy Commissioner, Mr. Peter Fitzgerald while expressing his concern at the rise in the number of attacks in Dublin; noted, "Parents especially have a big responsibility to know where their children are and what they are doing". The attacks were a two-edged sword, he said. Young people were the victims, but in many cases they were the perpetrators, too.

The position and role of Parents in controlling the violence of young people in today's society is an increasingly difficult one. For instance, Parents are increasingly concerned about the impact of television and particularly television violence upon their children. Little work has been done on the subject in Ireland but studies carried out all over the world clearly show that this concern is well justified. It is important, however, to put television in its proper context as only one of many influences for good or evil upon children. It is equally true that television can have a beneficial impact depending upon the quality of programmes, which young people watch.

That being said, the findings about the impact of television violence are alarming. In the first instance the amount of such violence in increasing. One study revealed that in the United States young people have viewed 20,000 acts of violence and 16,000 murders by the time they reach eighteen years of age.

Not only is television violence increasing it is also more realistic, frightening, blatant and bloody. Unfortunately very young children are unable to distinguish between real and television violence. This is also true of less academically able children who are inclined to watch more violent programmes and spend longer watching television than their peers. There is a significant link between the impact of television violence on children, their belief that it is realistic and the amount of violent programmes they watch.

This is compounded by the fact that society itself is becoming more violent. Hardly a week passes without a murder or violent incident being reported in the Irish media. Such a state of affairs did not exist twenty or thirty years ago, which means that television violence is now more compatible with what is sometimes shown on the news. There is a danger that children may see violence as normal in society and this view is strengthened by television violence.

As insidious factor is that some violent acts on television are seen as justified where the 'baddie' gets his comeuppance. Young people (and adults) take comfort from this and violence, therefore, is soon as an acceptable way of redressing wrongs. This is often part of the staple died of cartoons, for example.

It is not surprising, then, that every study shows a strong link between television violence and aggressive behaviour. This link is seen in children as young as three, by which age they will watch a show designed for them

95% of the time. But research has shown that the eight to twelve year old group is the most vulnerable. What is seen as crucial is the total amount of television watched. It is almost like the cumulative effect of exposure to the sun leading to skin cancer. One expert studied a group for twenty-four years, from when they were eight to thirty years, and found that those who watched a lot of television were more likely to be in trouble with the law in later years.

Some of the more undesirable influences of television violence are that children become less sensitive to the pain and suffering of others and less bothered by violence in general. They are more likely to strike out at play-mates, argue, disobey authority and be less willing to wait for things. Their view of the world may become distorted and it may be seen as a mean and hostile place. Television may also teach new ways of violence.

All this is a genuine cause for concern and this concern is added to by the availability of horrific videos and the arrival of the Internet. But, are parents helpless? It is true that they are isolated from each other and lack the type of communal support their children have at school or discos. This, nonetheless, does not mean that parents are powerless. It is well to again recall that they ultimately exercise a very powerful influence on their children by their example in general in how they relate with their family, with others and how they solve problems.

The exercise of parental authority is a legal and moral right and is obviously fundamental. It is our duty as parents to protect our children in every sense, including prevention from over-exposure to violent or unhealthy television programmes or videos.

Parents can decide how much television their children watch, they can ban watching violent programmes, obtain electronic locking devices to block them, monitor a few episodes of a particular series to check that the series as a whole is acceptable. Common sense dictates that parents should begin this process when their children are young, rules about viewing should be fair and consistent and should obviously change as the children grow older when they are given more responsibility and may, perhaps have a television set in their own rooms.

A balanced approach is important and includes recognition of the value of television, encouraging children to watch good quality programmes, discussing programmes, realising that programmes with a caring theme have been shown to have a very beneficial effect on children. Finally, as parents we should be conscious of our own viewing habits; it has also been show that watching television in the presence of children increases the impact of such programmes on the children.

Television violence is a relatively new phenomenon which parenting

has to take into account. But parenting was never, and never will be, easy. One set of problems may replace another, but parental influence will continue to be decisive and lays the foundation in children for a balanced or otherwise adulthood. **August 28th 2000**

*   *   *

Shareholders' revolt only way to get fair deal from Eircom

Nearly half a million people bought shares when Eircom floated in July 1999, making it the biggest public offering of stock to hit the market in Europe last year. The flotation succeeded in bringing the concept of stock ownership to the masses in a way never seen before in Ireland. With one in five adults in this country holding shares, it is fair to say that Eircom is definitely not an ordinary company.

On September 13 the company will hold its first AGM (shareholder's meeting) as a public company. It promises to be an interesting meeting for a number of reasons.

The company has had a rocky first year as a publicly traded corporation and has controversially coughed up handsome bonuses for directors despite its poor performance on the stock market. Eircom stock, which is trading at approximately £2, has shed 33% of its value since the company went public.

The revelation of extravagant salaries, large bonuses and perks given to Eircom's top executives at a time of heavy losses for its shareholders is bad enough. But the news that the same fat cats are seeking even greater rewards is indefensible.

Long suffering shareholders will be asked to approve a generous options scheme for them at the company's AGM.

Eircom shareholders should attend the meeting and vote against the package. Every penny given to the board comes out of shareholders' pockets. Details of the directors' salaries make painful reading for those shareholders nursing 33% losses on their investment. Even more galling will be the list of directors' shareholdings exposing the lack of confidence and commitment from nearly every board member. The directors failed to put their money where their mouths were, preferring to use their huge salaries for other investments.

Unfortunately, it is likely that the generous incentive options scheme for senior executives will be passed at the AGM. The larger shareholders, the so called institutional investors such as the banks, building societies, fund managers and insurance companies will cast their votes in support of the board, come what may. This will thwart the wishes of the huge numbers of shareholders at the meeting.

It will be interesting to see if the trustees of Eircom's Employee Share Ownership Trust (covering the Eircom employees' 14.9% stake in the company) approve the incentive options scheme at the AGM. Indeed, it will be quite ironic if the trustees vote in favour of the scheme, especially as the majority of trustees are trade union representatives.

Whichever way the individual institutional investors vote, they have certainly been vocal on the fat cat issue, while the trade unions have been generally quiet. The Communications Workers Union (CWU), in particular, has been ducking for cover.

However, there is no doubt that Eircom's senior management is feeling the heat of public outrage. In an unusual development, the company's chief executive, Alfie Kane, wrote an apologetic piece in one of the Sunday papers. Regarding Eircom's low share prices all he could offer was his concern and the well-rehearsed jargon about changes in the telecom business and also that Eircom shares were overpriced at the time of flotation. Conveniently, this was the Government's fault.

Predictably, Alfie Kane does not explain why he didn't say at the time of flotation that he thought Eircom shares were overpriced.

Regarding the contentious incentive scheme he wrote: "A long term incentive scheme is being proposed to shareholders at the forthcoming AGM. You could ask why there is the need for such a scheme, and whether it is in the interest of the business and shareholders. It is, in fact, usual for PLCs in Ireland, including all our competitors, and PLCs throughout the world to operate such schemes to attract, motivate and retain key people."

In other words, the scheme is essentially about loyalty and staff retention. However, it was reported in the same paper that £287m spent on productivity schemes at Eircom in the last three years may have been largely wasted.

Though the company incurred the costs of laying off 1,600 employees during the period, it has recruited as many people as it let go.

The most bewildering aspect of Eircom's executives' proposed share options scheme is that it is unclear what price Alfie Kane and the other senior executives will have to pay should they decide to exercise their share buying options. It's unlikely to be anywhere near as high as the flotation price paid by the public for shares.

For instance, if the share options were set at the current price, Mr Kane and his colleagues could reap more stock and wait for better days precisely because the shares have under performed.

To her credit, the Minister for Public Enterprise, Mary O'Rourke, has shown flair and courage in deciding to oppose the directors' greed. She is being consistent. In April 1999, when Eircom was still under her steward-ship, she forbade Alfie Kane and his colleagues from writing themselves a generous options scheme, despite immense pressure from them.

In many ways, it is unfortunate that the highly successful privatisation of Eircom has been soured by the behaviour of its board and management. It is now a company whose consumers are unhappy and whose shareholders are miserable, while its management is vastly enriched. Its behaviour is damaging not only to the small shareholder but also to future privatisations.

The taxpayers' other assets, like Aer Rianta and Aer Lingus, are being devalued by the Eircom experience. Alfie Kane should realise that there are times when saying sorry is not good enough. **5ᵗʰ September 2000**

*　　　　*　　　　*

Government can make fuel tax cuts without upsetting the EU applecart

With the exception perhaps of electricity, there is hardly any commodity that we are more dependent on than the fuel refined from crude petroleum. Therefore, when oil prices rise by over 35%, we are all affected in one-way or another.

It is estimated that hauliers who rely solely on diesel transport £250 million worth of exports every day. As consumers it is hardly surprising that many in this country watched the pictures of crippling blockades in France with apprehension. Yesterday morning motorists in Brussels faced a similar city centre gridlock blockade by Belgian protesters. Similar protests in Britain over the weekend have led to panic buying at petrol stations in North Wales and Northwest England.

After a week of intense diplomatic pressure from the US and European policy-makers, ministers from the 11 nation oil cartel, OPEC, said they would add an extra 800,000 barrels a day, or 3% to world production.

However, energy analysts warned that while the deal which was more generous than expected should prevent oil prices from rising further, it was unlikely to reduce them significantly in the short term.

Last week, oil prices hit a post Gulf War high of $34.50 a barrel. Lawrence Eagles, an energy analyst from the firm GNI Securities, doubted the OPEC decision would bring down prices to less than $30 and warned that planned closures of European refineries for maintenance would keep petrol prices up by reducing supplies.

OPEC has blamed heavy duties imposed by western finance ministries for the high petrol prices.

"We think this is enough but we want consumer nations to work to reduce taxes," said Qatar oil minister, Abdullah bin Hamad Al Attiyah.

Here and in other euro zone countries, paying for dollar denominated oil with an ever-weakening currency aggravates a painful situation.

With the train strike still fresh in our minds, it is doubtful anyone would welcome disruptions from the Irish Road Haulage Association. However, it is extremely difficult not to sympathise with their point of view and ponder the positive effect on the high inflation rate if as the hauliers demand Government duties on diesel and petrol were reduced.

Although world oil prices have skyrocketed in recent months, imposing severe strain on the economies of all industrialised countries, the proportion of the Government's excise duty and VAT on the average cost of litre of petrol or diesel is staggering. According to AA (Automobile Association) figures, the average cost of one litre of unleaded petrol is 76.7p. However, the price breakdown is quite revealing; the production cost is 28p, the wholesaler makes 2p, the retailer makes 4p while VAT and excise duty rakes in a whopping 42.7p (over 55%) for the already bloated Government coffers.

The scenario is similar for diesel. The average cost is 68.49p, but the VAT and excise duty payable is 37.49p, which is over 54% of the cost.

Despite conflicting signals, it is likely that any tax cuts for PAYE workers scheduled for the next budget will be shelved.

Presumably, this is because the prevailing view is that such measures may push up our inflation.

It is reasonable for the Government to consider introducing alternative measures that will help tame the spiralling inflation rate as it continues to bite at 6.2%.

Finance Minister Charlie McCreevy would be well advised to think twice before ignoring growing union demands to reduce the impact of inflation on the living standards of ordinary people.

Although the EU Finance Ministers meeting in France over the weekend warned against tax reduction on fuel while conveniently pushing for price reduction by the oil producing countries, it is ironic that the French Government agreed to make fuel tax reductions only a few days before the EU meeting. The French may have unwittingly created an irresistible precedent for other EU governments.

In any event, reports indicate that Irish taxes on petrol and fuel oils are substantially above what EU tax harmonisation rules require.

Charlie McCreevy insists that the spiralling inflation rate is caused by external factors outside his control the surging price in oil and the weak euro.

Obviously there is some merit to his argument and with oil prices at their highest rate in 10 years; it is heartening to here that Taoiseach Bertie Ahern will meet with the Irish Haulage Association tomorrow.

But the Government has the latitude to make the required excise duty reductions without infringing EU directives. EU minimum duty directives allow the Government to charge up to 25% less than the current excise levels, which represent just over half the current price of diesel.

Hopefully the latest announcement from OPEC signals a drop in oil prices in the medium to long term. In the short term, it is imperative that the Government introduces decisive measures to prevent any industrial unrest, while insulating the consumer from incurring any more crippling increases as a result of the high oil prices. **12th September 2000**

*   *   *

Budget must open doors to affordable housing for all

As we eagerly await the budget speech next week, a survey released yesterday by Focus Ireland shows that the number of people on local authority waiting lists has increased dramatically.

Urgent political action by the Government is required to tackle this matter in the budget for the next financial year. With the economy continuing to boom, and affordable housing continually becoming a mirage for thousands, now is the time to use the budget surplus to reduce the local authority waiting lists.

The survey reveals that the total number of applicants for council homes has risen to 45,645. This represents an increase of 17% on the previous year.

The number of people on local authority waiting lists was just 26,000 only four years ago. However, in the current climate of spiralling property prices and rapidly increasing rents, it is inevitable that many more individuals and their families will be forced to seek secure and affordable accommodation from their council.

A significant number of those among the new applicants for council housing have been young couples who have failed to get a toe on the property ladder. Traditionally, these were the people who bought starter homes with the intention of trading up to a better home as the years progressed.

It is scandalous that local authorities are being forced to spend millions on land before even digging the foundations. One local authority, Dun Laoghaire Rathdown, has just paid nearly £3m for two acres of land. It is estimated that this will put a £100,000 price tag on every site.

It is pointless pumping extra millions towards housing if it is going to go straight into the hands of land speculators.

Accordingly, there is an urgent need for an expansion of the Compulsory Purchase Order Scheme to address the problem. It has been alleged that some landowners pushed up prices when it became common knowledge that a local authority was interested. Councils are often perceived as having a bottomless pit of funds.

In Cork the problem is so acute (more than £400,000 per acre has been charged in some cases), that the corporation has effectively abandoned efforts to purchase sites for local authority housing.

Cork Corporation is pioneering a programme whereby entire private housing estates are purchased en bloc directly from the developer. One scheme already purchased in this manner, comprising of 24 three-bedroom homes off Cork' s Old Youghal Road, will dramatically ease the housing waiting list. The Corporation has confirmed that, until suitable land becomes available within the city boundaries, this policy will be pursued and expanded.

Donegal County Council set a new record earlier this year when it paid out a staggering £375,000 for two and a half acres of land in Ramelton, six miles north of Letterkenny. The cost of the development, at £150,000 an acre, is indicative of the challenge facing the local authority as it attempts to acquire a land bank in order to tackle a housing waiting list predicted to exceed 2,000 applicants by the end of the year.

"We have to pay market values which are escalating monthly and these vary depending on the level of interest in the site," explains Senior Housing Officer, Gerry Gilroy. Senior Housing Officer with Sligo County Council, Joe Gethins, confirms the council has been forced to pay up to £100,000 an acre for land close to the town. In Galway city, the corporation is paying up to £500,000 an acre for local authority housing land.

Obviously, the most important objective in resolving the crisis is to increase the supply of available housing. Just how many new houses per annum does the State need anyway? It was thought, two years ago, that 46,000 housing units a year would fit the bill. But even though that number was built, in 1999, the total demand has since grown to 50,000.

The total spent on new houses in 1999 was estimated at £6,267 million, an increase from £4,541 million the previous year. However, this 27% growth in value terms has been predicted by the ERSI to slow to

22% this year. Instead of increasing to meet demand, it seems the housing supply growth rate has been steadily decreasing.

This runs counter to what the National Development plan called its key priority of increasing social housing output. The plan has indicated that over the next 10 years, the output required will be "well in excess of 50,000 units per annum."

The plan has also suggested that Ireland's housing stock of 327 units per 1,000 of population, compared with the EU average of 450 per thousand of population, is the lowest in the EU. This indicates the extent of catch up required, irrespective of demographic forecasts, which suggest that the Republic's population could reach six million in the foreseeable future.

If the Government were genuinely committed to addressing this major shortcoming, one would expect that their incentives would not be restricted to first time buyers. Instead they would try and encompass all levels of the housing market. The stamp duty of 9% for non owner-occupiers, as recommended by the third Bacon Report, has been universally criticised.

The new rate, depending on individual house values, is up considerably. In many instances the duty has effectively doubled.

This disincentive, together with the new annual tax of 2% per annum on the value of residential property not occupied by owners (except in designated areas), may eventually have a catastrophic effect on the private rental sector.

Many economists warn that these measures will reduce the supply of rented accommodation and push up rents. The Auctioneers' Institute has rightly pointed out that the government should have initiated incentives that would attract private investment into the sector rather than providing obstacles that will keep them away.

Given the huge budget surplus, it is imperative the government acts positively in the forthcoming budget on the supply side of new housing. There is a pressing need to ensure that there is an adequate stock of serviced land in public ownership so as to get housing plans speedily into effect with the use of private contractors.

Additionally local authorities should move to purchase private dwellings to house people on their waiting lists. **28th November 2000**

A WORLD OF RELENTLESS CONFLICTS

With 40 years experience in UN peacekeeping operations, Ireland's entry to the UN decision-making executive, the Security Council, is well deserved. It has been gratifying to learn from the Taoiseach that our representatives will adopt a reforming approach during our term, in line with proposals from UN General Secretary Mr Kofi Annan. I would also hope that the UN Security Council will benefit from Ireland's expertise in conflict resolution and peacemaking.

Conflict resolution in Afghanistan will be the first test for the Irish representatives. Late last month, just before Ireland joined the Council, the committee voted for tougher sanctions against Afghanistan as punishment for sponsoring terrorism and harbouring Osama Bin Laden, the alleged mastermind behind the 1998 bombings of two US embassies in East Africa. With rare concord, both the United States and Russia have agreed to isolate Afghanistan to halt instability caused by Islamic extremism. But, in a big region marred by stubborn little wars, simple sounding sanctions promise to turn 2001 into a complicated year.

Set to begin later this week, the sanctions appear more symbolic than serious. Afghanistan is already among the world's most inaccessible places. But it remains a destination for the guns of war, the drugs that buy them and the fighters who soldier for causes often far removed from the ills of this ravaged land. Exasperated politicians, who can't stop the region's terrorists, have made Afghanistan into a diplomatic voodoo doll, swapping periodic pinpricks for the difficult work of brokering peace.

The US and Russia insist that the sanctions will be effective because they target the Taliban, not Afghan civilians. But punishing a repressive military movement will inevitably affect those living under it. Such insensitivity has led Kofi Annan to admonish the Security Council for victimising civilians and compromising the United Nations' persistent, if faltering, search for peace.

At the height of the Cold War, the Soviet Union's underbelly was mapped as an arc of crisis. Although times have changed, the mind set has stuck. The arc of crisis is now treated like an arc of frustration. Recent reports, prepared by the CIA's National Intelligence Council, depict all the major regional players in Afghanistan's war in colours of ethnic fragmentation, religious militancy and geopolitical instability. The sanctions have demonstrated that symptoms have taken precedence over causes. The hard won experience of other wars has simply been ignored.

While the sanctions suggest that isolation will push recalcitrant Taliban leaders to the bargaining table, they also suggest that such isolation will inspire Afghans to rise up against the Taliban. On the one hand, the UN seems to be suggesting that sanctions might lead the Taliban toward multi party democracy. On the other, they suggest that central and Southwest Asia will only be safe from extremism if the Taliban disappears altogether. They assume that multi-party negotiations will lure reconstruction funds to save the struggling economies of Afghanistan's neighbours, but think little about which of the region's autocrats and meddlers might be empowered if money floods in.

The sanctions reflect a puzzling ambivalence toward Afghanistan's war. Russia, Iran and Central Asia still support General Ahmed Shah Masoud's tattered Islamic Front army against the Taliban. But only enough to sustain fighting not win a war. A strict arms and fuel embargo, applied to all suppliers and combatants, is desirable, practical and possible but endorsed in word only. Instead, sticks are offered as carrots. Stop drug trading and we'll resume talking. Hand over Bin Laden and we'll resume talking. Treat aid workers better and we'll resume talking.

Spontaneous rebellion? Bribery? Enlightenment through decree? These are fantasies, not policies. It's little wonder the Taliban misinterpret most messages.

Wars are stopped when guns, fuel and fighters are in short supply. Yet no one has stopped the thousand-mile long arms bazaar that radiates from Afghanistan and Pakistan. Inequity, inequality and repression feed wars. Yet almost no one wants to invest the energy to protect human rights in Afghanistan or in its increasingly oppressive neighbours. Preaching peace through punishment can' t work if the same states that are advocating sanctions are participating in the war, if only by proxy.

When there were real chances to end the Afghan war in 1989, when Soviet troops withdrew, in 1991, when the communist government fell, and at several junctures since no one cared enough. Thus, fighting spread far beyond Afghanistan's boundaries.

Today, Afghanistan's borders are more important than Afghanistan itself. Central Asia worries about its future stability. Pakistan is anxious about a political and economic implosion. Russia, India and Iran worry about energy security and the US is increasingly worried about being blown up by former Afghan fighters. Everyone is worrying about territorial sovereignty. No one, it seems, is worrying about Afghanistan.

It took most of the world far too long to understand that what happens in Afghanistan affects all its neighbours. But the Security Council has learned the wrong lesson from this as it has from the conflicts surrounding Sierra Leone and Congo. Rather than try to stop the war by sanctioning the war's suppliers, it has censured the Taliban for its war's nasty spill over. Only when the focus returns to ending the Afghan war will any chance for success emerge.

Maybe the astute diplomats from the Foreign Affairs department at Iveagh House can make a real difference and persuade the Security Council to tackle the arms suppliers? Until then, men in suits will continue to dictate terms to men in shawls, and neither side will understand the other. Fighting will continue and people will die. **16th January 2001**

* * *

Calm is crucial as the Middle East threatens to explode into chaos

All wars are cruel, some are senseless and a few qualify as insane. Insane wars bear no heed to the costs involved or the issues at stake. They feed on hatred instead of personal calculation or national advantage. The Israeli Palestinian conflict is rapidly slipping into this category, just as peace seemed within reach.

With the expiry of the ultimatum issued by the Israeli Prime Minister Ehud Barak last night and his accompanying threat to scuttle the entire "peace process" the situation in the Middle East is now at a dangerous and delicately explosive juncture. Doubly dangerous is the fact that the Palestinian Israeli citizens—a million or so in all in Israel proper have, for the first time since 1948, joined the protests on such a scale and with such violent results.

Hatred has overtaken the hope that Israel's Prime Minister Ehud Barak sought to nurture, with his visionary peace offers to the Palestinians at Camp David this summer. His proposal for the Palestinians to regain most of East Jerusalem and to call it al Quds, the capital of a Palestinian state, was intended to restart the stalled peace negotiations. It was completely overshadowed by the brazenly provocative visit of Israel's opposition leader Ariel Sharon to the holy Islamic site of Jerusalem, Mr Barak' s refusal to join the Palestinian leader Yasser Arafat and Madeleine Albright at last Thursday's summit in Egypt, and his rejection to permit a genuinely neutral international investigation into the causes of the latest violence.

Naturally, Sharon claims he did not set out to provoke Palestinian violence. But it is clear that he did nothing to avoid becoming a pretext for the predictable upheaval that followed. Sharon has offered the equivalent of a manslaughter plea: he suggests that he played into the hands of Yasser Arafat and his lieutenants, who, he claims, have in fact orchestrated much of the violence for their own political effect. Sharon styles himself a fool rather than a knave. The political space that Barak hoped to create for himself and for peace is being squeezed out of existence by such extremism.

Despite all the pictures we have seen from the conflict in the last few days, it is disappointing that we have not seen any of Arafat going on Palestinian TV broadcasting to appeal for calm by the Palestinians. He has let the fires stoked by his Fatah youth organisation burn without interference. Perhaps, if the leaders on both sides had acted differently at the outset of the crisis, the odds are that Mohammed Aldura (the hapless 12 year old Palestinian boy shot by Israeli soldiers) would still be alive. The same is probably true for most of the more than 80 others, mostly Palestinians, who have died as well.

In that sense these deaths are not random or senseless. They have meaning. They are the cost of political acts that appeal to hatred as a tool of political gain. Arafat seeks the world's sympathy and diplomatic advantage from these deaths. Sharon thinks his macho swagger will bring him votes. But the force of hatred, stirred by such slaughter, quickly overtakes calculations like these. Senseless behaviour edges into the insanity of revenge at all costs. Israelis and Palestinians must find a way out, by finding a way to avoid that unfortunate outcome.

Now, the violence must stop. No new magic ingredients are to hand. In order to bring about a political settlement of the conflict between Israel and the Palestinians the genuine grievances and aspirations of both sides must be taken into account. The history of enmity cannot be ignored, nor can the historic attachments to holy places or the respective security and economic interests of the two communities.

Violence is not the answer, nor is the perpetuation of inflammatory myths by both sides.

What is needed is the utmost restraint on the Israeli side. For the average Palestinian there are several unresolved issues that need to be tackled urgently. Under the terms of previous peace agreements with American blessing and brokerage, it was agreed that there was to be a trade off: the Palestinians would get their land, or most of it, in exchange for peace with Israel. But it has not worked out. Most of the land remains in Israel's hands or under its effective control. Illegal Israeli settlements have continued to expand, especially under Ehud Barak. Jerusalem remains the strongest contention not just the holy places but the Arab neighbourhoods and areas.

There remain major restrictions on Palestinians' freedom of movement, access and right to reside in Jerusalem impositions reminiscent of the Pass Laws of apartheid South Africa.

It is a story of continuing dispossession, occupation, humiliation and oppression, and cruelly lowered expectations, all the more bitter given raised hopes of peace. Israel' s leaders, for the most part, cannot see beyond a hostile Arab population who must be contained and controlled, even if it means overriding Palestinian civil rights and self-determination.

There has been continual failure to recognise that the Palestinians are (to an almost pathetic extent) the weaker party. Despite the commendable role of President Clinton in the peace process, it is unfortunate that the international community has not been able to provide an honest broker (that is truly independent of either side) for the bargaining process.

At the end of the day, the Palestinian and Israeli interest lies in achieving an honourable peace accord as soon as possible, so that both peoples can channel their immense human energies into a better life for all.

It will be an unmitigated disaster if Mr Barak's ill-advised threat to scuttle the entire peace process becomes a self-fulfilling prophecy. **10th October 2000**

*   *   *

People's unity best weapon against defiant Milosevic

It is unheard of anywhere in the world for a dictator to listen to the voice of his people and leave quietly after receiving a devastating electoral defeat. If ever one has had a compelling interest in staying on, it's Slobodan Milosevic, Yugoslavia's strongman of 13 years, the mastermind of four ethnic wars who is accused of war crimes against humanity. Suddenly the man who successfully depicted himself as at one with the Serb people has lost his aura of invincibility with the stunning admission that he came second in last week's presidential ballot.

Despite the extraordinary significance of this victory for the Opposition, this is only the beginning of a delicate and uncertain battle to reap the fruits of their well-deserved victory and force Milosevic out of power. According to the official results announced by the State Election Commission, the margin of the Opposition' s victory fell short of the majority required to avoid a second round run off set for October 8.

However, it's unclear whether a run off will actually take place. The Opposition's presidential candidate Vojislav Kostunica and his followers are refusing to accept the commission's tally and have organised a nation-wide strike.

The Opposition has also planned rallies but this kind of strategy has failed in the past. While people are galvanised by an apparent election victory, that enthusiasm could vanish within the winter months.

The strategy of the Opposition is based on the hope that Milosevic will leave office voluntarily, bowing to international pressure (if Russia were to join the chorus) and growing discontent at home, especially between traditional Milosevic allies, like the police and army. But he has shown no intention of resigning. There is no indication that he is losing support among his top allies. But that may change rapidly, especially if hundreds of thousands of people join the campaign of civil disobedience and strike.

Why did Kostunica not accept the deal of a second round most analysts believe he would win easily? It's because the Opposition thinks the second round is a Milosevic trap which could allow him cancel the contest altogether.

It is now up to the people they are the ones who will decide the course of events in the coming days, not the politicians. In the past demonstrations have not frightened Milosevic. What he saw was a cheering crowd celebrating a victory he does not even recognise. This is not a crowd that threatens him.

Kostunica's rally last Wednesday went ahead with the permission of the interior minister who asked for the event to be moved from Parliament Square to Republic Square. This is an indication that Milosevic still thinks he can win this battle, undeterred by Western calls to step down.

But if Milosevic sees hundreds of thousands or even a million people responding to opposition calls for a countrywide strike, the mood could change rapidly. How the President reacts depends on the numbers a successful strike will show him that people really are fed up. How the security forces react depends on the number of protesters. If demonstrations swell it is possible that neither the police nor the army would have the guts to intervene.

I really doubt that the army will turn their guns against children in the streets and the police are sick of breaking up demonstrations. This time they would be doing it with the certainty that Milosevic is no longer the most popular politician in the country.

But is violence really the only way out of this mess? Kostunica wants to avoid confrontations with the police and he must know by now that the majority of the people are behind him. They trust him he promised changes and he will do all he can to bring about those changes but this does not mean he needs people to be beaten up. Before the elections, Kostunica said that he did not expect rapid changes. He said these elections would be the beginning, a turning point.

He knows this is a marathon not a sprint and if his supporters are beaten back right away the demonstrations may come to nothing. That would be the end of the game for him. After all, something vital has already happened here. Milosevic and his allies admitted defeat, albeit partially. Nobody here expected that even hours after the polls closed.

Kostunica may embark on a long political struggle against Milosevic's regime. The Opposition controls more than 100 towns, including Belgrade, and next year there will be elections in the Serbian Republic.

If the Democratic Opposition of Serbia remains united it may win and put further pressure on Milosevic to leave power without any bloodshed. **3rd October 2000**

*   *   *

The remote control TV world of American foreign policy

With the US Presidential election at a critical stage, Vice President Al Gore and Governor George Bush are preparing for a final debate tonight, which could be a decisive factor in the outcome of the election in three weeks time. With the Middle East on a knife-edge and fireworks elsewhere, it was expected that foreign policy issues would dominate the second debate last week.

Perhaps we should not expect too much foreign policy detail from a Texas governor who refers to Nigeria as "an important continent."

Yet despite that gaffe, George W Bush seemed not only to hold his own but he set the agenda during an extended discussion on foreign policy that took up half of the second presidential debate.

So why should we care?

It's a foreign election after all on the other side of the Atlantic. American voters really don't care about foreign policy anyway. After the Cold War, it appears that Americans now are living through the sort of quasi isolationist period that typically follows a big war. In fact, the famous button question "which candidate would you trust to be in charge of the nuclear button?" Is not often asked of today's candidates.

Ah, but weren't we jerked awake the day after Wednesday's debate when Middle East violence was renewed including a terrorist attack on a US Navy warship? Suddenly we were reminded that in the uncertain and fast changing post Cold War era, purposeful and strong leadership from the only surviving superpower is in everybody's interest. Given the close relationship between the Irish and American economies, it is obvious that if the American economy sneezes, the Irish economy will catch cold.

Thousands of jobs in this country are tied directly to the success of the American economy and its volatile stock markets. Therefore self-interest alone makes it difficult for us to ignore the US elections.

By their nature foreign affairs are complicated and far away, and unfortunately American voters seem to be telling their presidential candidates that they don't want their brains to be taxed by too much thinking. Vice President Al Gore's polling numbers declined after the first debate as he was widely criticised for appearing to be too arrogant about his own knowledge. It's one thing to be smart; it is another to shove it under people's noses. As a result, during the second debate, Gore was less aggressive to the point of being apologetic during those instances in which he actually acknowledged some disagreement with Bush.

With that in mind, it was significant to hear how few differences there were in their most exhaustive airing of foreign policy views. Both men showed themselves to be internationalists to the point of being interventionists, but they each stopped short of detailing the circumstances in which they think this mighty nation should intervene in international conflicts.

In the last decade, neither President Bush nor President Clinton developed a clearly stated, comprehensive foreign policy agenda. The elder Bush did try New World Order during the Persian Gulf War, but that raised more questions than it answered, especially among those who are paranoid in the US about government power.

The younger Bush introduced another novel term during the last debate, "humility." Bush wants more of it and, surprisingly, Gore agreed. Never mind that during the debate Gore called America "the natural leader of the world" because of its military and economic might. I must confess that I missed the humility in that remark.

Apparently, Bush frets that America is too often seen as arrogant and unilateral, a valid point. Thankfully, on that point, Bush departs from Clinton and Secretary of State Madeleine Albright's description of America as "the indispensable nation." Bush may be following the model of his father, who successfully enlisted important allies before engaging in such big overseas adventures as the Persian Gulf War.

The younger Bush offered America's "vital interests" as a standard for American intervention, but in reality US troops tend to go where the television cameras go. TV pictures of starving children lured the Bush administration into Somalia, for example, with the support of then Senator Al Gore. But the operation crept from a rescue mission into an ill-fated national endeavour that accelerated when the Bush administration yielded power to the Clinton administration.

Bush also called for early warning systems to avoid tragedies like Rwanda. At least half a million unarmed civilians were slaughtered there in about three months in 1994 because the US, and other major world powers, ignored repeated early warnings from the United Nations commander there and from Belgium. Sadly, it took TV pictures of the slaughter to awaken the Clinton administration.

Clearly, neither candidate appears to have a well thought out or clearly defined comprehensive foreign policy agenda. This is ominous if the past is anything to go by. The failure to seriously think about international tragedies of the past and formulate imaginative foreign policy initiatives by a country that is powerful enough to implement the same, effectively means that we are doomed to repeat them, unless the rest of the world, particularly the EU and the UN, is prepared to take a less US dependent role on the international stage. Most likely, we will have to wait until after the elections to find out what the course of American foreign policy will be. I have a good guess: just follow the cameras. **17th October 2000**

*   *   *

Getting rid of Mugabe the only way
Zimbabwe can end the nightmare

History may be in the making in Zimbabwe. Never has an African head of state been forced by a combination of civilian protest and parliamentary impeachment proceedings to leave office before his term runs out.

It seems that with the right leadership from opposition parties however, the demonstrators who stormed the streets of Harare last week may have the power to force President Robert Mugabe to stand down.

It is a prospect that Mugabe has brought upon himself. His own cynical disregard for the democratic process has left the opposition with little choice. Any hopes that the ruling Zanu PF party' s narrow victory in elections last June might jolt Mugabe into reconciliation and economic and political reform has been dashed. Even in the face of defeat his determination to stay in power, at least until his term expires in 2002, seems undiminished.

He has pressed ahead with a ruinous land resettlement policy. He persists with a futile and costly involvement in the Congo war and has made a mockery of justice by giving amnesty to the thugs who intimidate the electorate and continue to harass the opposition.

Despite new faces in the Cabinet he has yet to come to grips with a dire economic situation. Inflation is running at an annual rate of 62%. The Zimbabwe dollar is sinking, foreign reserves are exhausted, tourism has collapsed, fuel shortages are expected to get worse and the full impact of the damage done to the country's vital commercial farming sector has yet to be felt.

Though it is impossible to predict when Robert Mugabe's 20-year rule will end, the events of recent days have made it clear that his Government's economic mismanagement will be his undoing.

Mugabe has already had a taste of what lies ahead. For three days last week demonstrators, angered by rising food and fuel prices, ran riot in the suburbs of Harare. So severe is Zimbabwe' s economic crisis that workers, in a population where more than half the national workforce is unemployed, can barely afford the cost of commuting to work.

Mugabe, who has been in power since independence in 1980, has tried to cling to office by ingratiating himself with rural voters and guerrilla war veterans. The Zanu party narrowly beat the MDC in a general election in June after Mugabe authorised the violent seizure of white owned commercial farms and condoned the murder and intimidation of MDC supporters. Urban Zimbabweans have voted overwhelmingly for the MDC. Their dissatisfaction with Mugabe and Zanu increases daily. Even if the Government can suppress public protests, it seems powerless to rescue what was once one of Africa's most successful economies.

Nevertheless, President Mugabe was up to his old tricks last week, declaring that the old white leaders be tried for genocide. Ironically, his 20-year hold on power owes a lot to the old white regime.

The former Rhodesian town planners were a wily bunch. They made sure that black slums were a long way from the centre of town. In the event of a protest a few roadblocks could stop protesters from coming near the seat of government. Mugabe, the man who overthrew the old racist regime, must be grateful.

As Zimbabwe' s President, Mugabe lives in the grand old buildings that white settlers vacated two decades ago. Like his predecessors, he is widely hated. Mugabe is as popular as a scorpion in a bathroom. A poll released on October 25 by the Helen Suzman Foundation has found that Zimbabweans disapprove of the Government' s handling of the economy. Three quarters of the population wants Mugabe to resign. Even Zimbabwean businessmen have called for a general strike.

The MDC has already started impeachment proceedings though the case against Mugabe is watertight so there is little chance of its success. Even before the motion reaches parliament that is dominated by the ruling party, the speaker, one of Mugabe' s closest allies, can strike it out. The best the MDC can hope for is to embarrass the President with a parliamentary debate on his personal defects. These include the persistent flouting of court orders, the flamboyant corruption of his relatives, and the use of presidential amnesties to free his hired thugs and the dispatch of 12,000 troops to a useless war in Congo without consulting the Cabinet.

Mugabe has responded to impeachment measures by threatening to prosecute those white Zimbabweans who fought him in the independence war. He has even named two senior MDC members, neither of who did any fighting. As bizarre as it sounds, he has also declared it time to revoke the policy of reconciliation between black and white citizens.

If the MDC fails to co ordinate urban protests, matters could turn violent. MDC members have already accused their leaders of cowardice for not mobilising the township crowds. But caution is in order. Mugabe is as cunning as he is ruthless.

Demonstrations alone may not be enough to bring down the President. A more strategic plan might be a combination of street protests and the decision by Government MPs to cross the floor. This would force an early presidential election. If the mood of the electorate is anything to go by, Mugabe will surely lose to Tsvangirai of the MDC.

Getting Mugabe to stand down will not be easy. Tsvangirai will also need to win over the military. He has to persuade them to support the fresh start that Zimbabwe so desperately needs. It will be a difficult and dangerous process. But there is one certainty: as long as Robert Mugabe remains in office, Zimbabwe's crisis will continue to deepen. **31st October 2000**

*   *   *

If hardliner Sharon wins, peace wrecker Arafat has only himself to blame

A new page is about to turn in the Middle East. Today, Israel is voting for a new prime minister. Opinion polls indicate that the peace-seeking incumbent, Ehud Barak, is almost certainly going to be rejected in favour of his hardline opponent Ariel Sharon, the man known to Palestinians as the Butcher of Beirut. It appears that Barak is being punished for failing to deliver peace, when the real blame should be on the Palestinian side. Regrettably, but predictably, Palestinian Authority Chairman Yasser Arafat responded to Barak's politically bold proposals with violence.

Barak used his electoral mandate and reputation as Israel's most decorated soldier to take bold risks for peace with the Palestinians. Sharon is not so conciliatory. Hated by much of the Arab world for his management of Israel's 1982 invasion of Lebanon and his complicity in the massacre of Palestinian refugees by Lebanese Christian militiamen in that same year, he would surrender only 42% of the West Bank. By contrast, Mr Barak was willing to surrender about 95% of both the West Bank and Gaza. It was Mr Sharon's visit to a disputed holy site in Jerusalem that sparked the latest Palestinian rebellion and caused the rupture in the negotiations.

Arafat may rue the day that he rejected Barak's peace offers and unleashed violence as a negotiating tactic. Israelis appear ready to respond by electing Sharon. The Palestinians will not get a better deal from Sharon. Indeed, they probably will see a return to the intransigence that characterised the Government of Likud's Benjamin Netanyahu, who was Barak's predecessor. They should brace themselves for more Israeli settlements in the West Bank, stricter Israeli security and a harder line against Palestinian gunmen and rock throwers.

It now appears that months of conflict between Palestinians manipulating the "children of the stones" and Israelis deploying the weapons of an army have returned the Middle East to the brink of violence.

It is a particularly uncomfortable time for those of us who had hoped that Barak would abandon the frustrations of step by step diplomacy and, with American support, lead Israel toward a comprehensive negotiated settlement. Unfortunately, many in Israel have accused Barak of offering unreciprocated concessions that recklessly endanger Israel's security.

The charges are grossly unfair. Barak and Clinton had been demanding different but politically matching concessions: from Israelis a bitter retreat on full sovereignty in Jerusalem and from Palestinians a yielding of their

3.5 million refugees' right of return. On the Israeli side, at least, any territorial changes negotiated by the leadership would then have to be submitted to a referendum.

Barak should not be dismissed for putting new chips into play. He earned credit for introducing considerations that must become part of any realistic deal.

True, Barak's tactical judgement can be faulted. He consulted inadequately and got too far out in front of his political base. Many of his supporters, let alone critics, acknowledge those deficits.

His principal error, however, was to put unearned confidence in Yasser Arafat, who has hung back from taking the necessary political risks.

In a sullen but relatively quieter past, Arafat was able to take some of Israel's no's for a temporary answer. But in the explosive context of renewed Palestinian insurgency, he was not prepared to take Israel's latest yes. These included Barak' s stated readiness to hand back a misshapen but improvable 95% of the West Bank plus the Arab neighbourhoods of Jerusalem for a rump Palestinian state. The offer was so serious it split Barak's domestic base.

Yet Arafat demanded more. Faced with a similarly heavy burden of Palestinian reciprocity, he showed no similar leadership responsibility. In what was no less than a call on Israel to commit demographic suicide, he rejected Bill Clinton's appeal to yield the Palestinians' right of return. He did so rather than undertake the admittedly difficult mission of bringing along his constituency. Instead he renewed the intifada.

It is impossible to say now when conditions will permit a productive return to diplomacy. Barak will be counting on something of an electoral miracle in the Israeli election today. Without such a turn in his favour, Israeli voters are left in the lurch of their own ambivalence between Barak and Ariel Sharon.

There are, of course, no Palestinian voters, only Arafat. President Bush cannot possibly have wanted to teethe on this issue and may reasonably ask for a time out.

With ragged low level conflict continuing and diplomacy in stalemate, perhaps it is time for temperature lowering alternatives to a formal negotiated solution. However, it is impossible not to consider whether the Mideast issue is ripe for solution or indeed soluble at all. With the election of the right wing Opposition candidate, Ariel Sharon, virtually a fait acompli, it appears that Israel stands at the edge of an abyss. Indeed, there are real fears that a vote for Sharon will mean the death of the peace process in Middle East. Ironically, in long drawn out conflicts, the greatest courage is often demonstrated not by the valiant warrior in battle but by leaders who have the fortitude to take risks for peace. **6th February 2001**

*   *   *

Ghana's vote of confidence brings hope to continent plagued by corruption

In the light of Africa' s tabloid of horror stories in recent years famine, civil war, carnage and destruction it' s excusable to cheer about good news the Western press often misses. Last month, Ghana carried out a successful democratic transition, closing the darkest chapter in its postcolonial history.

The 19-year rule of Jerry J Rawlings, who seized power in a 1981 coup, was often marked by brutal repression and extreme cruelty. Although the retired flight lieutenant often stated his contempt for multi party democracy, intense domestic and international pressure compelled Rawlings to organise elections in 1992. He ran for president, arguing his 11 years in office should not count toward the two-term limit he wrote into Ghana' s Constitution. He won, but electoral irregularities were so widespread that opposition parties boycotted parliamentary elections for four years. The result was a one party state.

Rawlings won a second election in 1996, firmly establishing the Rawlings model of self-succession in West Africa: a military adventurer seizes power in a coup, organises fraudulent elections to ward off nosey Western donors and returns to power as a "civilian president". West Africans call this "civilianisation of military rule". By 1998, military despots had shed their uniforms for civilian clothes in 10 West African countries.

Ghana's economy was the chief victim of Rawlings' rule. A self styled Marxist Leninist revolutionary, Rawlings imposed heavy restrictions on commerce and the economy. By 1982, more than a million Ghanaians had fled to Nigeria.

Unable to secure help from his friends the Soviet Union, East Germany and Libya, Rawlings went knocking at the door of the World Bank and the International Monetary Fund, which he had denounced as imperialist. Seduced by his charisma and rhetoric, and the chance to snatch Ghana from the Soviet orbit, the West poured in billions. The World Bank pumped more than $4 billion into Ghana, declaring the country the "economic star of Africa" in 1992. But by 2000, Ghana' s economy was again in a coma and the World Bank sponsored Economic Recovery Program a miserable failure.

Inflation stood at 60%, unemployment hovered around 30%, interest rates had reached nearly 50% and Ghana' s currency, the cedi, had virtually collapsed. Before Rawlings took power in 1981, the foreign exchange rate was 2.75 cedis to the dollar and income per capita was $410. In 2000, the exchange rate was 6,800 cedis to the dollar and income per capita was $360.

At least 40% of World Bank and IMF loans and Western aid was squandered. The regime, which preached the World Bank gospel of accountability and transparency, never accepted responsibility for its failures, choosing instead to blame foreigners and external factors for the country's worsening economic crisis. Ghanaians, however, never accepted Rawlings' claptrap. Fed up with corruption and years of economic mismanagement, they vowed electoral retribution at the polls, scheduled last December. But Rawlings was determined to hang on to power even at the risk of implosion.

His reluctance to relinquish power is all too typical in Africa and helps explain why the continent is rife with collapsing economies. The abortion of the democratic process plunged Angola, Chad, Ethiopia, Mozambique, Somalia and Sudan into civil war. Manipulation of the electoral process destroyed Rwanda and Sierra Leone. The subversion of the electoral process in Liberia set off a civil war in 1989 and instigated civil strife in Cameroon, the Republic of Congo, Togo and Kenya in 1992.

The military's annulment of electoral results sparked Algeria's civil war the same year and plunged my home, Nigeria, into political turmoil in 1993.

This pattern was recently repeated in Ivory Coast, which had been the bastion of stability and prosperity in a region wracked by carnage. Last October, Ivorian junta leader General Robert Guei, who had seized power in 1999, stood for election. When early returns showed he was losing, Guei sacked the electoral commissioner and sent in his military goons, armed with bazookas, to take over the vote count and declare himself the winner. Angry Ivorians drove Guei out of office. He fled the country, leaving behind chaos.

Mindful of this, Ghanaians greeted their elections with anxiety. Blocked by the Constitution from seeking a third term, Rawlings had hand picked his vice president, John Evans Atta Mills, to be his successor. Though marred by violence, the vote count was generally fair. The opposition New Patriotic Party won 97 of the 200 seats in parliament, but since none of the presidential candidates won over 50% of the vote, a run off was scheduled. On that day, Rawlings unleashed his military thugs. Roadblocks were set up to prevent voters from going to the polls. Commandos beat up suspected opposition voters.

When the results started coming in, the opposition candidate, John Agyekum Kufuor, held a comfortable lead over Mills. Would the ruling National Democratic Congress relinquish power? Of 190 African heads of state since 1960, only 20 gave up power voluntarily.

When Mills telephoned Kufuor to concede defeat, the country heaved a collective sigh of relief. Ghana had managed to pull itself back from the brink, thereby bringing to seven the number of African countries that have made a democratic transfer of power from one elected president to another. The other six are Benin, Botswana, Mali, Mauritius, Senegal and South Africa.

To the Western press, such a peaceful transfer is no news. But it was great news in Africa. Perhaps, no news is good news, after all. **13th February 2001**

ABOUT THE AUTHOR

Wole Akande, a former Columnist with the Irish Examiner, is a freelance journalist and a qualified lawyer. Ireland's first Black Columnist; he currently works in the Hi-Tech industry. He is married with a child.